There was a moment when I believed my journey was at its end...I lived to tell my story.

Live to tell yours.

First Edition: October 2023

For inquiries or permission requests, write to the publisher at the address above or email at contact@donnykkeiko.com

TABLE OF CONTENT

Introduction

Dive into the raw and riveting memoir of my tumultuous childhood, marked by adversities that would break the spirit of many. Yet, through these pages, my resilient spirit emerges, one that refuses to be diminished by circumstances.

From confronting personal life battles to battling societal expectations, each chapter is a testament to my journey, punctuated by moments of profound pain, fleeting joys, and monumental growth. The narrative doesn't just dwell in the shadows, though; it's a triumphant story of how one can plant seeds of strength in the most infertile grounds, nurturing them with hope, love, and determination to bloom against all odds.

This is not just a memoir; it's an inspiration, a lesson on how even in our darkest moments, we have the power within to rise and shine. As you turn each page, you'll be invited to reflect on your own journey, recognize your seeds of strength, and be reminded of the incredible resilience that lies within us all.

Join me on this unforgettable journey and witness the transformative power of hope, grit, and the sheer will to thrive.

Share snaps of your favorite pages, memorable quotes, and moments from this book on social media with #donnykkeikobook, tag me, or post it on your story! I'd love to like them and spotlight them on my profile!

CHAPTER ONE

A Childhood in Africa

Not only that many people tend to view Africa as a place filled with difficulties and hunger, but they also imagine it as a place with daily struggles. However, through my eyes, I view it as a place where the sun always shines bright, along with the most beautiful looking plants, and with one of many of the freshest fruits and vegetables you can ever find. Here, love is the language everyone speaks while your neighbours treat you just like family. There's always going to be a feeling of home around every corner.

I was born on a sunny day in May 2001, in Gaborone, Botswana. My mom held me with a joy that lit up her entire face, her dream of having a baby girl finally coming true on her fourth try. I was lucky to be greeted by three older brothers who loved me from the start. Let me tell you about Benjamin, who was just over a year old when I came into the picture. He wasn't just a brother, but quickly became my best friend, always watching over me with a kind of curiosity that only little kids have. Our mom would remind him to be gentle, saying, "She is delicate".

Benjamin couldn't get enough of potatoes, especially when they were served with African dishes. He'd constantly ask Abby for "potatoes", and with my arrival, he found a new buddy to share his favourite treats with. Throughout my childhood, one of the most treasured memories was the experience of sharing meals with my siblings. It was more than just eating together, it was an experience that solidified our bond, creating moments of unity and understanding that have remained with me over the years. This simple act become a foundation for our familiar ties, a testament to the strength and warmth of our relationship.

Not too long after I was born, I was taken under the wing of my Aunt Abby, a sweet and loving lady who stepped in as a mother figure while my own mom focused on her studies. In our family, everyone pitched in. My oldest brother Mweeka acted like a second parent, with Chimufa and Benjamin playing their parts too. We were all around the same age, which made our home a lively and happy place.

Growing up, my brothers were my guides, teaching me everything from new words to how to walk. They were always there to help me explore the world around us. At the same time, young Aunt Abby was finding her way in life, but she never let her personal goals interfere with taking care of me. Mweeka, who was wise beyond his years, became my main caretaker, doing everything from changing diapers to putting me to bed at night.

In Zambia, we have this colourful cloth called chitenge. It's a simple but strong fabric used for many things, from head wraps to baby carriers. Abby used to carry me on her back with it, keeping me close and snug while she did her house chores. I'd often fall asleep to the comforting routine of her day, especially when the aroma of home-cooked meals filled the air. So, amidst all the bright colours and warm bonds of family, my journey began, woven with threads of love, learning, and growing up in the heart of Africa.

My mum and dad didn't talk much about their marriage, but from what I saw in my early years I could see the love slowly fade from their faces. My mum met my dad when she was in her late teens, in Zambia. He was from a different tribe, and they came together. He supported her during her school years learning how to become a nurse. My Mum is a soft-hearted person, she cares deeply about people, and I believe she doesn't have a bad bone inside her, unless you get on her nerves or do wrong by her. I started learning how to talk and the language I spoke was Tonga and Bemba, I spoke it fluently. I was a young girl in Zambia telling my brothers to stop chasing me with bugs, running around with my strong little legs, and going into the bushes Abby told me not to because I was adventurous.

I didn't wear shoes; I felt the earth better this way while I was on my adventures by the river or climbing trees to pick mangoes. There was a sight of a mango and it looked bright and juicy, me and my brothers' set eyes on it while we were out on our bikes searching for fruits. When I caught sight of it, I slowly got off my bike, turned to my brothers following behind me and pointed to the mango and said, "I want to grab this one". They looked at each other in surprise and looked up at the tree. Mweeka the oldest suggested I didn't climb as expected. Chimufa had the biggest grin on his face and cheered me on while I ran towards the tree. I looked up high in the sky with my tiny body and realized the height was too much, I looked around for a broken stick. I finally found a good enough stick that could knock down the glorious fruit, then asked Chimufa for a lift up to the tree branch.

He walked closer with his hands out prepared to launch me up. I was finally up in the tree after struggling for a moment, I looked down and a slight sense of fear came to me when I realized how high I was sat on the branch. I leaned over with one hand holding onto another branch and the other with the stick I found poking at the Mango. I tensed my face in struggled as I realized I was just touching the Mango but not close enough to give it a powerful knock. I shuffled over some more and leaned as much as I could, extending my arm in hopes to give the mango a good knock. I finally managed to hit the mango enough to make it fall off the tree and just in a second, I lost balance and fell to the floor with my brother's reaction time trying to save me from falling it was too late I already hit the ground.

Lucky enough I didn't land on my head which would have caused a much more severe injury than the graze I got. Tears filled my eyes, and before I could start crying, Chimufa bent down beside me and said, "you say you're a big girl, and big girls don't cry. We won't be here forever, so get up." He stood up and watched as I slowly stood and wiped my tears away, then they all gathered to hug me. That walk back home stays in my mind whenever I face tough times. At that moment, I learned I could hold back my tears. When we got home, Abby had a meal ready for us - my favourite, Nshima and chicken, a real treat. In Africa, we grow our own food and raise animals, which makes meals even more special.

One day, I was playing barefoot in the garden, looking in the bushes for something to play with. Abby would warn me, "Don't go too close, there might be snakes!" but I would ignore her and keep searching. I knelt down and looked

9

carefully until I found what I was searching for. I waited a moment, then grabbed quickly, catching a snake by its head. Happy and proud, I ran back, arm raised and a big smile on my face, shouting, "I got one, I got one!" Benjamin ran out, clearly impressed. He always loved studying creatures and animals in great detail. He looked at the snake, then smiled at me, saying, "I know exactly what type of snake this is." Amazed, I asked, "How?" He then told me about the snake, using its colour and size as clues.

The exciting past few weeks made me forget that I hadn't seen my mum for a while. Time seemed to fly by, and it was making me a bit confused. I didn't call Aunt Abby my aunt anymore; she was my mum now. Even though I knew my real mum had left, Abby was always there, looking after me every day. She was my home. My mum left when I was just a baby, bravely choosing to follow her dream of becoming a nurse. She did well in school and got a job in the UK. In Africa, people often look for opportunities abroad, not because life here is bad, but because it's hard to get ahead, whereas the UK offers more chances. Abby told me to be proud and that she'd be back soon. My dad was still with us, but he was always working to save up money.

Our house was small, but it was cosy. We could talk to our mom on the phone, each taking turns to tell her about our day and our little adventures. When it was my turn, I didn't know what to say, other than that I missed her and couldn't wait to see her again.

In early 2002, my mum boarded a plane, her belongings packed in a suitcase, heading to a small two-bedroom house in Lancaster, UK. Although the house was a bit rundown, to us, it was a new beginning. Working two jobs was hard, she had very little time to rest, but she always kept a smile on her face. Every night, she'd have her meal, Nshima, her favourite dish, while looking at photos of us. It made her happy and a bit sad, but she knew why she was doing it. My dad joined her in 2003, and together they worked hard to save up enough money for our future. Back home, we stayed with Abby, and even though both my parents were away, I didn't feel sad. I felt safe and loved with Abby, holding her close as I slept peacefully each night.

We love to dance in Zambia; it's a way to express joy and celebrate. I stood on the grass in a pretty red dress, ready to dance at our home by the lake. My uncle set up a DJ set that a family friend sent from the UK. The music blared from the speakers, playing songs stored on a CD. Our neighbours joined the garden party, and we danced and danced. Sitting on a car tire that we used as a chair, I sipped water from a cup that Abby handed to me. As I looked at the happy faces around me, I realised that happiness is truly found at home, and I was right there, at home, where I belonged.

Chimufa was a character we'd say. He was outgoing, bubbly, he spoke to everyone he met with a huge smile on his face, his heart was pure, he was young and full of enjoyment, when he was around his energy was infectious. If a room was silent and he was present he'd be the one to stand up, clap his hands and say "right, let's all play a fun game!" And everyone would cheer up. He'd be the one to smile when

11

things got hard, I didn't see him cry, or share a sign of weakness in my presence, teaching me strength was his most valuable thing to do. He knew how cold and unsettling the world was and I was his "little sis".

He often referred to me this way instead of my name, he only called me by my name when he was angry or frustrated with something I had childishly done. My heart filled with joy when he would walk into the room and say, "hey little sis what are you doing?". He always wore shorts and an oversized T-shirt; his hair was always cut down short and he didn't like to grow it out.

CHAPTER TWO

Navigating a New World

One day, he came home from school with a dog with him, that dog became a big part of our family, it had colour fur spots all over it, I was young so playing with the dog was exciting, I'd attempt to ride the dog like a horse and giggle as I fell off. I was blessed in life to experience a lovely lady called Regina, she was skinny and wore her Afro short, she loved warm weather and wine, and worked hard. I called her my grandma even though she was an aunt to my mum. She was close to my heart and anytime I needed her for emotional guidance she was my safe space. She wasn't soft like other grandmothers; she was hard core but really soft inside. I loved spending every Christmas with her she made it so special to me. When she also left to the UK for her second time, I missed her so much. This was the first time I ever experienced someone I loved so much leaving and it hurt but I knew I would see her soon. She also worked in the health industry in UK.

She's the one who helped my mum in the first place, and we always stayed grateful for it. In Africa everyone is your guardian we each do our part in helping one another for whatever it is that's needed help with, I loved that about home. The day was finally coming, the moment I'd leave my home and say goodbye. My mum had flown to Zambia thrilled that after years of working and waiting the time had arrived and her babies could finally be with her. My brothers were excited. I looked under the bed and seen our dog scared, I waved my hand to try reach him, but he was too far deep under the bed, so I gently asked him to come out of the bed. He slowly came out the bed and I squeezed him. "I'll miss you" I said holding onto him. I believe dogs have a sense of understanding to humans, I knew he knew we was leaving, I comforted him until Abby said, "it's time to go". My parents had a home in Zambia, they decided to sell it to accurate more money for the relocation, everything started to feel so real. The plane journey was very exciting, it was a new place, a new start, I didn't know what to expect.

I remember the first day of being in the UK. It was cold, my hands were frosty, my mum had bought me a coat with red patches on. It was quite big, the sleeves went over my hands and I loved it, I felt snugged. I hadn't learned English yet so communicating with anyone other than family was quite hard. My dad had taken me to Morecambe, a seaside town where the beach was, but it was never really hot enough to enjoy it, I still appreciated it though, it was nothing like Zambia or Botswana. We got out my dad's small blue Peugeot and walked to the arcade. It was magical. My eyes lit up, it was a new world, I stood and froze, the music, the colours, the kids, the games, I looked around in shock. My dad was holding my hands and I let go to quickly run around, "what does this do?", "can I play on this" I was running out of breath with excitement.

He looked so happy; he knew all the effort it took to bring us to the UK was paying off in that moment. We took a photo, and I kept that photo for years to come. When it was time to go home, we stopped by an ice cream van by the seaside and took a stroll down the promenade. "How are you liking it so far" my dad said looking down at me, I replied "it's cold but it's so fun" I said eating my ice cream and

shivering to keep my body warm. The reality was, it wasn't as cold as I felt, my body

was adjusting and I was so young it felt extremely cold, the weather was 15° that day

but to me, that was really cold. My dad could speak fluent English, better than my

mum. In fact, you would have never thought he grew up in Africa. He could spell very

well, and he adapted himself amazingly.

My parents had been in the UK for much longer than us, so they were used to

everything, we were still learning. We went home and me and my brothers sat by the

dinner table, I slapped my hands on the table making sounds impatiently waiting for

my dad to come into the kitchen. He had bread behind his back and walked in "this

is a treat" he said smiling. He waved the bread in the air, and we all looked at each

other confused "what is it papa" I said asking him in confusion. He opened it and

pulled a slice out and put it in the toaster. It was a magical moment when he buttered

it and cut it up in pieces and gave us all a piece. "It's so tasty" we all agreed and

asked for more. That night I went to bed with my tummy full of lovely warm toast. It

was so simple yet so significant to me, I cherished these moments of joy because it

was a new journey. Me and my brothers all shared a room, and my parents had their

own private room next to ours.

The corridors were small and tight, the bathroom was close by which was

handy. Even though it was a small house, it was special to me, the houses in the UK

were amazing compared to the houses in my hometown Zambia so I learnt how to

appreciate it. My dad spoke fluent English, even more proficiently than my mum. You would never have guessed that he grew up in Africa, given his impeccable language skills and seamless adaptation to the UK lifestyle. Since they had lived in the UK for much longer than we had, my parents were accustomed to everything here, while we were still adapting and learning.

I was just 5 years old when I arrived in the UK, so I wasn't attending school yet; I was in nursery. Benjamin was in primary school, while both Mweeka and Chimufa were in secondary school. Fortunately, their English was present but somewhat broken, whereas mine wasn't great at all; I could barely speak it. My mom dropped me off at nursery, and as she spoke with the teachers, I noticed that everyone looked significantly different from me. Their hair was straight in ponytails, while mine was braided with beads at the end. They had light, pale skin, and mine was dark brown. I clutched my mom's hand and hid behind her in fear. Not only was it a new country, but it was also new people! "Hello, little madam," Mrs. Henrinson said, kneeling down to match my height. "It's okay; the children here are very nice. I will introduce you to them," she said, extending her hand and gesturing for me to come with her.

I held her hand as she led me to the big, intimidating crowd of children. "Listen up, everyone, we have a new girl starting," she looked down at me and asked me to say my name. I didn't understand what she was saying, so I turned to my mom, and she translated for me. I proudly spoke my language, replying, "My name is Doniwe." From that moment, I knew things were becoming real, and I had to become a strong girl for my mom. My mom left for work, and it amazed me how she looked after patients all day on her feet, cooked dinner, and then took care of her babies too. I admired her for it when I grew up, but as a child? Not so much.

I was a shy child, and not speaking English made things even more challenging. I didn't talk in class and often had my head on the desk. I didn't raise my hand to answer questions, and honestly, I had no clue what was going on. During playtime, I enjoyed hanging around the bench and table area outside with crayons and paper, my juice box beside me, and I was content. My mom would always braid my hair for school, using different styles and colourful beads. It had been a long time since I had my Afro out, and I guess she did it to help me fit in as much as possible. One day, my mom came to pick me up from school, and she was holding my hand. I stared at the pavement as we walked, and when she stopped to talk to one of her friends on the street, I didn't lift my head. Slowly, signs of early anxiety began to show. My mom asked me to lift my head, but I refused. I didn't want to look at the woman in front of me. "She's shy; don't mind her," my mom said, laughing with the lady she was talking to. I let out a big sigh of relief and kicked my feet while waiting for her to finish. The entire way home, I didn't speak, in fact, I didn't speak for the entire week. I was selectively mute, only talking to my brothers. I wouldn't speak to anyone throughout the day, come home, go to our room, and sit on the floor with Benjamin as we played with our pens, imagining them as characters.

After playing for a significant amount of time, I went to use the bathroom and peered through the gaps in the staircase handles, leaning forward to see my parents at the table. "She's not talking to me," my mom said, upset. "She hasn't said a word

17

this entire week," my dad replied. I could sense that they were distressed by my anxiety; they didn't know what it was, that it was a real thing, especially that their daughter could experience it. "Maybe she's finding things hard," my mom said. "Of course, she is, she's just a child. I told you we should have waited until we put her in nursery!" My dad said, raising his voice. I quickly ran back to the room with my tiny feet, holding in my urge to use the bathroom.

The following day was a weekend, my favourite day! Saturdays had always been my favourite day of the week. The sun beamed through the window, waking me up, and I hopped over Benjamin, who was still sleeping, and ran to my parents' room, jumping on their bed. "Wake up, wake up, wake up," I repeated, excited for the day ahead. I ran downstairs, opened the drawer filled with pots, placed one on the cooker, and cracked the eggs. I was only 5 years old, but I could cook on my own. Many people might find it concerning, but in Africa, it's normal! I made breakfast for the family and sat down at the table, waiting for them to come. "Wow, you're sharp this morning," my dad said, being the first one to come downstairs. He picked me up, hugged me, and then sat down in his chair, ready to eat. "So, how are you today?" he asked, trying to start a conversation with me. "Well, I'm okay," I said, staring at the plate full of food I had cooked. I could feel him staring at me with concern, but my brothers came running down the stairs, filling the silence. "Thanks, sis," Chimufa said. "Thanks, Don," Benjamin said. "Yeah, thank you," Mweeka said, following last, walking down the stairs respectfully. We all ate breakfast, and I pulled my stool from the stove to the sink, starting to do the dishes. Doing chores was just a part of my routine; my parents didn't need to tell me to do them since I was so used to it in Zambia.

I started primary school and still hadn't learnt all the key English words. A few months in, the head teacher consulted my parents about my slow progress with language. They had a meeting with my parents, where they all sat down. "She isn't a quick learner," Mrs. Pie said. My parents looked at each other, and my mom said, "She's trying her best," reassuring Mrs. Pie while holding my dad's hand tightly. Mrs. Pie sat closer and asked, "Do you speak English at home?" My dad replied, "She speaks Tonga, Bemba, and Setswana in our household," with pride. My mom, confused, questioned, "What does this have to do with it?" "Well," Mrs. Pie explained, "the thing is, her development is significantly slow due to the different languages spoken at school and at home. We recommend that you completely stop speaking your languages and stick to communicating in English with Doniwe." My mom gasped, saying, "She's just a child! She will learn the language if you give her time. How can this be fair to our baby? Please take extra time to teach her in school," she pleaded, tears welling up. "Unfortunately, our teachers' main focus isn't teaching simple English words," Mrs. Pie said bluntly, showing no remorse.

The meeting ended with my parents being silent on the way home. When they introduced this new way of living, it upset me. I missed home; it was hot, the kids understood me, the neighbours were kind, and we played together. The UK was nothing like that. On top of that, I had to change how I spoke. I ran upstairs to cry; everything began to get overwhelming, and I couldn't handle it anymore. It took me a

19

while to adjust to the new way of living, but the best part was that I made new friends named Annabelle and Megan. They were in the same year group as me. Megan lived at the bottom of my street, and Annabelle lived on the street beside mine. It was convenient for all of us to go to the park at the end of the street. The street was on a hill, which was cool because we could create makeshift carts out of bins, sit in them, push each other down the hill, and scream in excitement. We'd take turns, even though it was dangerous; it was extremely fun. We would hang out at the park for hours, and when dinner was ready, Annabelle and Megan would head home, while I remained on the swing, waiting for my friends to return. When they did, I continued playing.

I often ate dinner late because I had to wait for my parents to get home. My mom would have Chimufa pick me up from primary school after he finished high school, and he would take me home. He had a close friend named Liam and Carl, and the three of them would walk beside me as we strolled home. When we got home, he would let me run down to the park and play, but he was young too, so he would hang out with his friends. "Did you have your dinner?" Megan asked me one day as she returned to the park. "Nah, I'm not hungry," I said, lying out of embarrassment. I was jealous of Megan; she had everything I wanted. She had a pink room, her own bed, her own space, she was the only child, her mom was always at home, making her the best meals. Her house was spacious, and she even had a play area. She had all the latest tech and the nicest clothes. Her bathroom was nice, and she had a beauty set too.

One day, when she gave me a tour of her house, I said, "Wow, you live in paradise," looking around. "Paradise?" Megan replied, disagreeing. We sat in her room, did each other's makeup with a top 100 songs of 2007 CD playing. We danced around her room, laughing while falling onto the floor and staring at the ceiling. "This is so much fun," I said, wishing I didn't have to go home. Megan and I were close, and Annabelle didn't enjoy it, but I didn't care. Annabelle was nothing like Megan; she was nice on some days but mean on others. She made mean jokes and played them off as if they were nothing. I hated how she made me feel, so I avoided hanging out with her as much as possible. Annabelle had a big dog, a Rottweiler, and it was very vicious. The dog wasn't properly trained and didn't really listen to anyone. Annabelle's house was small and compact like mine, so I related to her when I visited.

I would make an effort to spend time with her, and most of the time, she was chill. The only thing I disliked about going to her house was the smell that came from the backyard. Her dog had used the garden as its toilet multiple times for weeks, and it was never cleaned. Annabelle said, "My mom doesn't get out of that chair to walk the dog", it made me realize how much her mum didn't care. I was shocked that there wasn't any concern for how the dog lived its life. When we walked past her mom, I noticed she had been there for a while, with empty beer cans and empty food trays everywhere. I started to realize that Annabelle didn't have a great home structure, which was probably why she acted out of character with us. I began to feel sorry for her; she walked home from school alone on some days, so I had my

21

brothers accompany her. One day, Annabelle's dog somehow escaped from her garden and ran away. We all tried to chase after the dog and find her, but it was difficult. We had no idea where the dog went or why it escaped. We asked her mum to help search for it in her car, but she didn't bother to get out of the couch, it made me frustrated.

CHAPTER THREE

Trials and Transitions

Annabelle and I grew closer because of this event, I understood her more. Spending time with Megan and Annabelle became one of the greatest joys in my life. We would all head to the local field and run until we were almost too tired to stand. There was a shop called 'Spar' on our street, and we would walk there and buy a juice carton with the little money we had. I never had enough to buy anything, so I would sneak around the corner and slip a pack of sweets into my pocket, then walk out, dipping my hands into my pockets to nibble on them. I was always ashamed to admit I didn't have enough money. In fact, it took a long time before I ever confessed to that. Some days, we would enjoy a stroll through the woods, which we were told were too 'dangerous.' I loved the woods; it reminded me of Africa, with bushes and bugs everywhere. I'd climb the trees and look out over the gardens of rich people's homes, sitting there and sneaking sweets from my pockets. "Wow, one day I'd love to live like this," I said, watching a child play on a swing in a big garden. "Get down from there!" Megan said, giggling. I jumped down, and we enjoyed the rest of our day looking at the cows and horses in a nearby farm field.

One day, Megan invited me to her home to play with her new toys. "What toys did you get?" she asked while unwrapping the packaging. "I didn't get anything. Is today a special day?" I replied. "It doesn't need to be a special day to get something," she said, revealing her brand-new toy. That evening, when her mum took me home, I

23

asked my parents for a gift, but they refused. I was young and confused, so I thought they just didn't care. The truth was, after paying bills, transportation, and childcare, there wasn't much money left. I stormed to my room in anger and found Mweeka sitting on the bed with his big Afro, reading a book. "Don't be mad," he said. The walls were thin so he could hear everything. "Why do you care?" I said, throwing a tantrum while opening my book bag. "Get a book to read and sit with me," he said, shuffling over and patting the space next to him.

I picked a random book and hopped onto the bed beside him. Everything went from chaos to peaceful in a split moment. He looked down at me and smiled. I eventually fell asleep, and he went downstairs to speak with my parents. He asked them to get me something small. The following day, my mum gave me a gift. I was thrilled to receive it; it was a mini bakery set. I played with it in my room while Benjamin played with his pens. His imagination was brilliant, and I could overhear him playing with the pen as pretend characters.

A few days went by, and Megan invited me to her house to play with my new toy. I brought it over to her place, and we played in her room. "Wow, is this your new toy?" her mum asked, standing by the door. "Yes, my mum gifted it to me," I replied. "Is it your birthday?" her mum said. "Ummm, yeah," I said in a panic. I wasn't comfortable telling people I couldn't afford things, and when she assumed it was a special day to receive something, I just agreed. I felt bad for lying to her, especially because she followed it up with my parents to wish me a happy birthday. My parents were confused and scolded me for lying. I didn't want to explain to them why I said it, so I just stayed quiet.

Winter arrived, and it was December 2007. Everyone was preparing for the holiday season, and the snow covered the streets. Going to school was now fun; my language skills had improved. At home, we only spoke English, even though I could overhear my siblings speaking our native language. "Hey, Miss," I said, taking my bag off and hanging it on the rail. "Are you looking forward to Christmas?" she replied. "Yes, I'm so looking forward to it!" I said, sitting at my desk. "Good morning," the entire class said in unison. The whole day, I was excited to head home and play at the park with Megan and Annabelle. When school ended, Chimufa was there with Liam, as usual. "Put your gloves on," he said, demanding that I keep warm. I huffed and puffed and put them on. "You can't go to the park today," he said. The Park was full of snow, and the streets were icy. "Can I at least go to Annabelle's house?" I said, and then he agreed to let me go.

He made me go home first and change out of my school clothes. All my brothers were back from school and were at home talking. I didn't care about what they were talking about; I was just excited to go to Annabelle's house. I walked over there to be greeted by tiny Annabelle. I looked over her shoulders and said, "Hello," greeting her mum sitting on the sofa. She didn't reply; she was too focused on what was happening on the TV. Annabelle escorted me to her room. "Look, I have this new CD for Christmas!" she said, putting a CD in the player. It played Christmas songs while we played with our toys. Annabelle was upset about me and Megan playing

25

together while she was grounded. I had told Annabelle that we still played, even though she wasn't allowed to play outside because we were bored, and we could always play outside when she wasn't grounded anymore. It was getting late, and I knew my brothers would be unhappy about me overstaying my curfew. When I walked out of her room towards the stairs, I felt Annabelle's hands on my back. "Hurry," she said, nudging me to walk faster. I was frightened of stairs; in Africa, I didn't have stairs, so it was a fear of mine I hadn't yet overcome.

After her second nudge, in a split second, I fell down the stairs. I blanked out in that moment; it felt like the whole world was spinning, and my head was hurting. I got up with my hand on my head, crying out in pain. Her mum turned her head and said, "Oh my gosh, are you okay?" I replied with tears, "No, I'm in pain." Her mum said I should head home and get some rest. I wanted her to take my hand and at least comfort me while walking me home safely, but she refused and said I didn't live far. I walked home alone on the slippery, icy pavement, slowly losing my breath. I reached my door and began panting. When I opened the door, I felt dizzy. "Are you okay?" Chimufa said, running to me. "I need to rest," I slowly said, losing my breath. Before I could even explain what happened, I had collapsed on the bed. My brother assumed I fell on the bed out of tiredness, so he tucked me in and went downstairs. My body started to shake, and white foam was forming in my mouth.

My eyes were rolling back, and I was officially having a seizure. It got worse over time, and the shaking led to me falling off the bed while continuing to spasm. My brothers ran upstairs after hearing the thump of my body hitting the ground. "Quick,

26

she's having a fit," one of them said. "Call Mum," another one said. "I'll get a towel," another one said. They all began panicking, unsure of what to do. My mum was at work, so she couldn't pick up the phone. On the third try, she finally answered. She immediately left work and rushed home. "Call the ambulance," Mweeka said repeatedly. In a few minutes, the ambulance came, and my body was still in shock. They rushed me to the hospital. My little body had severe trauma from falling down the stairs headfirst, leading to me falling into a coma.

I don't remember much from being in a coma, only that I was seated in a chair, surrounded by endless white light. There were no walls, no objects, and no other beings. I couldn't move, talk, or do anything; I just sat there. I had no sense of time, and honestly, during that time, I couldn't distinguish what was real from what wasn't. My mum sat beside my bed, and my brothers waited in the guest area. My dad came rushing into the room, asking, "What happened?" while grabbing my hand. My mum explained what happened, and he became infuriated. "Why didn't Annabelle's mum walk her home or make sure she was okay?" he said in frustration. "I spoke to her on the phone her mum said she looked fine," my mum said. "How can my child fall down the stairs and be fine?" my dad replied. They argued over my little body lying there until Mweeka came in. "I think you two need to relax and have this conversation outside," he said. My parents went outside to talk while Mweeka held my hand and put his head on the hospital bed. "Come on, little sis, please," his voice said, breaking.

I was in a coma for six months, and time seemed to fly by. The doctors were unsure about my recovery. The day I finally woke up felt like re-entering the world. The hospital room was filled with colourful balloons, and my family was all there. My mum talked about how she prayed for me and knew that "God would come through." I spent the next few days with nurses assisting me to the washroom; I couldn't physically move myself. Eventually, the hospital discharged me, and my dad was the one who came to take me home. We sat on the grass outside the hospital and took a photograph. He was so happy to have his little girl back home, and I was so happy to finally be home too.

Mweeka was a strong character; I used to see him as the glue holding our family together. He was the oldest, so many responsibilities fell on him, even though he was still a child himself. He had to grow up quickly because my parents were always arguing or too busy working. Just because they had their disagreements from time to time didn't mean they didn't perform well. They still paid the rent and put food on the table. I'm an emotional person, so as a kid, I needed more than financial support; I needed love. I got it from my brothers. They taught me almost everything. I had stabilisers on my bike wheels to keep me steady, and they taught me how to ride my bike properly. I fell a few times, but they always said, "Get up and try again!" I looked at my brothers as my saviours; in difficult times or struggles, I only wanted them. I came home crying one day because a child at school was calling me names. "Monkey girl, monkey girl." Her name was Ellie, and she was my first bully. I was really scared of her, and every time I saw her, I felt intimidated. She made fun of everything

28

about me and singled me out. When I told my brothers about it, they advised me to call her names back, but I was too afraid, so I allowed it to happen.

Physical education was my favourite time of the week. I was obsessed with sports, and in the running races, I'd beat Ellie and cheer in happiness. I didn't have the courage to be mean back, but I loved beating her in sports whenever I had the chance. In the changing room, some of the girls started wearing bras; their bodies were developing, and some even started their periods. But mine hadn't come yet. Ellie made fun of me for not wearing a bra. It made me insecure about my body; I hadn't felt insecurity before that day. The next week for P.E., I made it my mission to wear a bra. I asked my mum to buy me one from Primark, and when she did, I stuffed tissue paper in it and wore my top over it. I went to school, and they laughed; I ran to the bathroom, threw the tissue paper from my bra into the toilet, put the seat down, and sat there crying.

My parents decided to move to Morecambe in late 2009. Our tenancy ended, so it was time to move. The new home was above someone else's home, which felt strange at first, but we got used to it. There were two rooms again, but now the difference was the boys were getting much older and their own space. "Why can't we have our own room?" Chimufa complained to Dad. "You get what you get," my dad replied, turning his back. I was the only girl, so I felt like I was getting in the way of their fun. They were older and could enjoy better games and stay out for longer. Mweeka even got a newspaper job and was earning money. Chimufa was in trouble at school for smoking weed, and Benjamin had his own friends now. We were far

29

from Lancaster, which meant I could no longer spend time with Megan. I hadn't heard from Annabelle since the stair's incident happened. My parents didn't want me to be her friend anymore, so they kept me away from her and her family. It was just me and Megan, but we were so far away. My dad drove me to Lancaster whenever he got time off work, which I was grateful for. He would sit in his car for hours, falling asleep while we played at the park. When it was time to go home, I'd get in the car, he'd wave goodbye to Megan, and we would head back to Morecambe.

All of my siblings and I attended the same school. When Chimufa was in high school, he caused trouble. He was the class clown and didn't listen to teachers. Even though he stressed the teachers out, they had mixed feelings about him. He would skip classes and hang out in the school field, smoking weed with his friends. Liam was there, of course. Liam didn't talk much, and when I greeted him, his replies were very short. I guess he was probably high and shy at the same time. The teachers called my parents in to discuss Chimufa being expelled from school, and they were disappointed in him. Every now and then, they would argue about his behaviour, but instead of simply talking to him about why he was acting this way and addressing the root of his problems, they took their anger out on each other.

CHAPTER FOUR

Navigating Challenges, Finding Strength

One day, all of my siblings and I were sitting in the front room, watching TV. It was a very small TV, so we huddled close to it. I could hear my parents screaming upstairs and looked back a few times, staring into the distance. Mweeka noticed my distress, so he put headphones on my head and played music on his MP3 player. He turned the music up to the max volume and smiled at me. He didn't let me touch his MP3 player, so I was content wen he did. He did this often, and I was always confused as to why. It was only later on that I realized it was to shield me from hearing the sounds of my parents shouting. The song played, and halfway through, Mweeka disappeared; he headed upstairs. Benjamin and Chimufa both stood up from the floor, so I took the headphones off. I could hear my mum screaming in pain, the sound was horrifying.

I instantly attempted to run upstairs, but Chimufa grabbed me to stop me; he didn't want me to witness anything. Mweeka came running downstairs and ran to the landline. He dialled for the police and told Chimufa not to go upstairs. My dad came walking downstairs and walked straight out the door. He got into the car and drove off. We stood by the door and watched him leave while Chimufa ran upstairs to check on my mum. She was in tears and in pain. He sat with her, rubbed her back, and asked if she needed anything. She shook her head and asked him to close the door. I wasn't allowed to go in, so Mweeka stayed with me and Benjamin downstairs and

31

comforted us, saying, "Everything will be okay." The police arrived, and Chimufa put the headphones back on me.

But I was angry and lost; I didn't want to listen to music. I wanted to know what happened. So, I sneakily took one side of the headphones off to listen. "They argue a lot," I heard Mweeka say. "I just saw him hit her with a belt!" he continued. I was in shock; my dad was never vicious or angry, at least I had never witnessed it. He was calm, gentle, and sweet. Why would he do such a thing to my mum? My brothers and I spent the next few days helping my mum with everything we could around the house. She left for work, and we all discussed why what happened, happened. I was too young to have an input, and the only thing I wanted to know was when my dad was coming back. We didn't see him for months. When he did come back, he didn't talk about it; neither of us did. We just moved on. My mum was madly in love with him; they were not good for each other, but she only saw the good side of him.

Funny smells came from the house downstairs, so my mum went downstairs to check. She knocked at their door, and when they answered, fumes of drugs and alcohol lingered. They played loud music and had a dog that barked all day and night. Soon enough, it was too much to live with, so my mum wrote a formal letter of complaint. My mum argued with the woman who lived below us. "There are children upstairs who are going to school," she said angrily. The woman shrugged her shoulders and slammed the door in her face. Even though the house wasn't the best to live in, we still enjoyed it. The room was a bit bigger than the last, and there was more space in the garden, even though it was shared.

My brothers and I dug a huge hole in the grass and covered it with bin bags and pebbles. Then we got the hosepipe and filled it with water, creating our makeshift pond. We searched for tadpoles in the lake, caught frogs and other fishes, and put them in our pond. The days of work were complete, and we stood there proud, until my dad came to witness what we had done. "What have you done? This isn't our property!" he said, yelling at us. He dragged my brothers by their ears and told them to get inside. He told me to go to bed, and my parents started arguing again. This time it was our fault. We felt guilty for the pond we had dug up because it upset our parents.

One night, I noticed my mum packing her bags when I needed to use the bathroom. I stood there, watching her without saying a word. She moved slowly, trying not to wake my sleeping father. I continued to use the restroom and ignored it. The next night, I noticed her doing the same thing. I didn't need the bathroom that night; I just wanted to see if she would be doing it again, and she was. "Mum," I said through the gap of the bedroom door. "Go to bed, love," she said, signaling me to stay quiet. I tiptoed back to my bed and fell asleep.

A few days later, my mum decided to do the school run, which was odd since my dad did it every day for years. She didn't know how to drive, so we took the bus. This was early, before my dad was due to get up for work. She brought two suitcases with her, and I asked her why. "It's for my friend," she said, smiling and softly rubbing my arm. We didn't stop by the school; instead, we stopped elsewhere. She left the bags in another house and took me to school. She did this for a week straight. "I can take her to school," my dad said over breakfast. "It's fine; you can get extra rest" my mum replied, looking for her hospital ID badge. My mum was secretly leaving my dad. I hadn't figured it out yet, but I soon did.

When I did, I was confused. I asked my mum why she would leave without telling him, and she said it was "for the best." She was always so soft and kind, joyful and happy, but with my dad, she was always crying, angry, frustrated, and tired. So, I understood. I just wanted her to be her happy self. My dad found out she had a new place, and he flipped. He was furious with her, feeling betrayed and annoyed. He had been very controlling with my mum, so the fact that she did something without his wishes irritated him. He smacked my mum across the face, and she pushed him. Luckily, Mweeka was home this time to stop the whole thing from escalating as it normally would. "Go ahead and leave!" my dad shouted, pointing at the door. Mweeka noticed me standing there, so he ran to his room, untangled the wires to his headphones, put them on my head, pressed play on the MP3 player, and told me to eat my crisps. I didn't take them off because he played my favourite song. Mweeka did his best to shield me from any pain, as if he had wrapped me in bubble wrap to protect me from family trauma.

My parents divorced, and it was tough. My dad didn't provide any help, and he moved to a completely new city. My mum was all alone with her four kids while still working her nursing job. Mweeka began to work full time while taking care of me. "Do well at school and have dreams, okay?" he said, with his hand on my shoulders.

When he wasn't looking, I'd open his drawer and steal some of his money. I spent it on myself, buying food at school and the shop.

Chimufa, on the other hand, was a little tougher; he didn't want to work for anyone. He wanted to be his own boss and run things his own way. He would purchase packs of treats for a pound each and sell them for five pounds at school. I didn't see my mum much, but the times I did, she was working. She always talked to me about how important it was to go to school and get good grades. She had a picture in her mind of what she wanted for her children, even though she wasn't really a part of our daily lives. She worked double shifts, morning and night, leaving us alone. When she was home, she was tired and would take a nap before heading back to work. "You're old enough to make food for yourselves," she'd say. We started making our own dinner, usually just cooking pasta or having leftovers from the previous day. I remember the night she bought me a flip phone. I had never had a phone before, so I was extremely happy. Everyone else was getting the latest blackberry phone, but I was so content and grateful. I just wanted to stay in my room all day play on my new phone. My mum taught me how to use it, play a song, and adjust the volume. Those moments were the best, just her and I.

My childhood was shaped by resilience, love, and the unwavering support of my family. We faced financial struggles, witnessed arguments, and experienced hardships, but we also celebrated small victories, cherished moments of togetherness, and held on to our dreams for a better future. The lessons I learned during those early years continue to guide me today, reminding me of the importance of perseverance, empathy, and the enduring bonds of family.

It had been a while since Megan, and I had hung out outside of school. I started to isolate myself because I missed my dad so much. When the school day ended, I'd toss my book bag on the sofa, dash upstairs to my bedroom, and begin drawing. It was my sanctuary. I became so skilled at art that I participated in school art challenges and won every one! My mom signed me up for swimming lessons after my persistent requests, and I couldn't wait to start. They were scheduled for every Wednesday, complete with a swimming cap and goggles. During these lessons, we would swim laps in the pool, and I could swim without getting out of breath. My swimming coach even suggested additional training and competitions, but my mom couldn't afford it. She mentioned that she'd think about it, but when we got home, I'd plead with her to let me go for the extra training. Her response always centred on focusing on my studies to become a nurse.

She believed it was the right path, as she had followed it herself. I tried to respect her decision, but my grades were poor, and my heart was set on art and those Wednesday swims. Regina lived in Carnforth, which was quite far from Lancaster, especially since my mom didn't drive. As summer approached and I had no concrete plans, my mom packed my suitcase and put me on the train to Carnforth. "Grandma will be waiting for you on the other side," she assured me. Even though I was young, traveling alone excited me more than it scared me. It felt like an adventure! When I arrived, Regina was there with open arms. "How's school?" she

36

inquired as she took my bag. "It's fine, but Mom won't let me go to swimming training!" I replied while holding her hand. She took me to the local market and told me to pick out a toy.

I appreciated her effort to cheer me up, even though she didn't have much. When we reached her home, it felt cosy and familiar, like her. She gave me biscuits and tea and sat beside me. "I'll pay for your swimming classes," she announced. I immediately hugged her with joy. A few days later, I returned home, excited to begin the swimming classes. I trained rigorously and grew close to my coach. I started competing in minor competitions and won medals. My mom was impressed by my progress, even though her work kept her from attending my competitions.

CHAPTER FIVE

Navigating Challenges, Finding Unity

Christmas Day was a bittersweet holiday. In the UK, Christmas was different from back home; it was more about gifts than Jesus. I had to adapt. In our hometown, we would dress in our finest clothes and head to church to celebrate with the entire neighbourhood. At school, kids discussed their Santa wish lists. There was a boy named Jamie with blonde hair who was always kind to me. He included me in the conversation and asked, "What about you, Donnie?" I stared blankly and replied, "I haven't made a list yet." The truth was, I wasn't sure if I would receive anything that year. It was a tough time for my mom, who could barely afford rent and childcare on her own, and our family back home was ill and needed medical attention, which meant they needed money. I didn't bring up the fact that the other kids had wish lists; I didn't want to add more pressure to my mom.

As Christmas approached, Regina travelled all the way to Lancaster to see us. She brought a large suitcase, which made us think she was moving in, but she wasn't. She unpacked wrapped boxes of gifts and created separate piles. "These are for Christmas; don't open them!" she said, laughing and rubbing my head as I hugged her tightly. She saved Christmas for us just by doing that. The next few weeks were challenging for me to resist the temptation of opening the gifts.

Christmas finally arrived, and I got to see what was inside my present. It was a baby toy, the most beautiful gift I had ever received. The baby had brown skin and came with a bottle and diapers. Benjamin got a water gun that he used to playfully chase me around the house, Chimufa received a new tracksuit set, and Mweeka got a book collection he had wanted. The snow fell heavily outside, and we built a massive snowman. In that moment, I realised that moving to the UK wasn't so bad after all.

The new year was here, and we were all excited, except Chimufa was absent. We assumed he was staying at Liam's house, so we waited for him. The countdown began, and we watched the fireworks outside while holding each other's hands. It was our tradition to pray in the new year, and Mum prayed passionately as the fireworks illuminated the dark sky. It was fantastic. The following day, Chimufa returned home with money for my mom. She didn't ask where it came from; she just thanked him cheerfully and hugged him.

The truth was, Chimufa had started selling weed to local people. It wasn't something he intended to do long-term; he just wanted to make quick money to help our mom. She had taken out a £5,000 loan to cover rent and other expenses, so Chimufa's cash enabled her to pay back the loan promptly. Everything seemed stable, all thanks to Chimufa stepping in to help. My mom was yet to discover what he was doing, and with her work consuming so much of her time, she wasn't around enough to realise the situation until things took a turn for the worse. One day, I was home alone with Benjamin, drawing in my sketchbook while he played with my phone, which we shared. There was a suspicious knock at the door, and we exchanged worried glances. "You answer it," he said. "No, I'm scared; you do it," I replied.

We went back and forth until we heard a voice say, "Police!" The knocking continued, and we slowly walked to the door and opened it. The police officer peered into the house and down at us. "Can I speak with an adult?" he asked. "She went to the shop," we both said simultaneously. Our mom had instructed us to say this if someone knocked at the door. She told us, "Do not open the door. First, look out the window. If it's anyone important, tell them I'm at the shop." The police officer explained that he would return in a few hours. We immediately called our mom to come back from work. She arrived just in time for the officer's return. "How can I help?" she asked as she answered the door in her casual house clothes. "Is your son Chimufa?" the officer inquired, holding a paper in his hand. "Yes," she replied, her voice filled with fear. "Is he okay?" she continued.

They had a lengthy conversation by the door until the officer left, and my mom leaned against the door, slowly sinking to her knees. "What's wrong, Mom?" Benjamin asked, trying to lift her spirits. Chimufa had been arrested that day after being caught selling weed. Her heart was shattered, and she blamed herself for not being around enough to protect him.

I watched my mom sink into depression as the days passed. She refused to go to work, and in fact, she refused to get out of bed. Benjamin and I had to wake ourselves up for school, get dressed, and walk to school while holding hands. After school, he would wait by the gate, and we'd walk home hand in hand. "Is Mom going

40

to be okay?" I asked, filled with worry. "Yes, she will," he said, offering me a

reassuring smile. My siblings always smiled at me, and their smiles provided me with

comfort. A single smile could make everything feel alright. We had all obtained our

citizenship and legal papers to live in the UK, but unfortunately, Chimufa couldn't get

his application approved due to his arrest.

  The court hearing was days to come, and my mum was a nervous wreck. I

never seen her like this. She was always strong and fierce and didn't let a thing get in

her way, so seeing her like this worried me. I headed to her room and stood by the

door before she greeted me to enter. I sat on her bed and looked at her and said,

"I'm sorry". She asked why I apologised, and I explained how it was unsettling to

witness her go through a tough period in her life. she sat up in her bed and held my

hand "don't you ever apologise to me for how things are, do you hear me" she said

holding my hand tightly and nodding her head. "Yes mum" I said quietly. "Do you

hear me?" She said with more bass in her tone. "Yes mummy" I replied more

confidently.

  We sat on her bed and spoke for hours, she didn't baby talk to me so I

understood about if things as an adult would, but she wouldn't tell me if something

was wrong. I'm an empath, I didn't know what this was then, but as I grew up I had

more of an understanding of it. Everything just… hurt. Life hurt; my feelings hurt. I

was rarely sad for anything that happened in my life, but I was sadder for other

people. I took extra time to notice how other people felt, and their emotions felt like they were soaking into me, and I would feel what they were feeling. My mum described it as having a "motherly heart". She expressed that she didn't want me to change as I grew up, I guess she knew how tough life was and how life events change a person's heart... not me, my heart grew stronger over the years to come.

Chimufa's court date had arrived, and I was sent to stay with my mum's friend along with Benjamin. Me and Benjamin came in a pack of two not by choice, by force! We didn't leave each other's side to the point family friends started to call us "the twins" and I loved it. I admired him, he was fantastic, him on the other side had a love hate relationship with me. I was his 'annoying little sister' and any chance he got to remind me, he would. He teased me a lot and was the type of person to be blunt and straight forward about everything, so his non-sugar-coating words affected me sometimes. We arrived at Angela's house - my mum's friend. It was lovely of her to welcome us with plenty snacks and games, it kept us busy for a few hours before we became bored.

Mweeka spent this time in the library reading books, studying for exams, or with his friends Andrew and Joshua. He didn't want to get involved with Chimufa's problems because it infuriated him, he was disappointed with his actions. It was fair for him to feel this way since he was the oldest and he had the responsibility to make sure we are all doing as we're told.

Luckily, Chimufa was released and was given community service, which he hated of course. When he arrived home with my mum, everything was peaceful. He wasn't scolded or threatened to have anything taken off him, my mum was simply relieved that her son was back home. My heart filled with joy when I hugged him, he ruffled my hair and squeezed my cheeks then gave me the biggest smile. I didn't want him to ever walk out the house again, I wanted him around at all times! Dinner was prepared by my mum, and we all sat in the floor with our legs crossed, held hands and closed our eyes. Mum always started our meals with a lovely prayer to grace the food she poured her heart into. We would then dig in and enjoy our food talking to each other about our day. Mweeka and Chimufa exchanged some disagreements about Chimufa's behaviour which was stopped by my mum "we all make mistakes you should forgive him" she said insisting Mweeka calmed down.

I understood why he was annoyed with Chimufa, he did his best to raise us into respectable people, and selling drugs was definitely not on his list for who he wanted us to be. Mweeka and Chimufa are 3 years apart in age, so they related to each other and had a great bond. Over the years I watched their bond break, which was upsetting to witness since my memories was them having the best time together with each other.

The street we lived on was scary, I heard stories about strange men walking around at night. I'd even witness people sat on the floor with no shoes on, and rough clothing, there was a murder that happened a few doors down, and people would fight on the streets. I always felt bad seeing people sleep on the street, as I walked home from school, I'd attempt to say hi, but I'd quickly scurry away in fear when they responded with silent growls and a piercing stare. Just as I was about to enjoy a cup of hot chocolate while continuing my drawing, my mum asked me to come from the kitchen and sit down. She called for my siblings to come downstairs and join us.

This was unusual, we hadn't done this before, it was the first. I adjusted my position in the sofa trying to make myself comfortable from being crammed with my siblings, "you're squishing me!" I squealed. "Please" my mum said silencing us. "This is serious. very serious," she said holding back her tears. I dreaded the next few words she was about to say, I was eager to know but at the same time scared. "What is it?" Mweeka said sitting forward. "Your grandma Johanna has passed away" she said softly. Johanna was my Dad's Mom, I only spent time with her back home, I had got so used to her not being around but hearing that she would no longer be with us hurt my heart. All five of us sat there in distress... silent with no words that could ever express how we felt. We grouped together closely and hugged each other tight.

It was our culture to have a little family gathering to honour and show condolences for someone's death. This was the first time I had to do this, and I was still a child. Family members were driving to the house and walking in with flours, cakes, food, and gifts, meanwhile my mum stood in the kitchen on the phone with one hand rubbing her forehead. The room was full of people sat down and standing all here to show their love and comfort, even though it was a sad moment, it felt like a cosy one. I glanced out the window to see blue car pull up to the house, I couldn't believe it. I stood up and ran to the door, swinging it open to find my dad coming out of his car. "Dad? Dad?" I repeatedly said with tears streaming down my eyes. It's all I ever wanted, him. His arms extended open, and I quickly ran to him with my little legs then he launched me into the air and spun me around. It was the warmest embrace, finally, he was home. He put me down and I grabbed his hand and took him inside, with my burst of excitement I had forgot what had happened and why he came in the first place. Everyone greeted him, shakes his hand and some cuddled him and wished him well. My mum on the other hand stood by the kitchen and waited for him to approach her. "I am so sorry about the news. The kids miss you" she said quietly. "Thank you, I miss them too" he replied. Their conversation was short and brief, when all the family members left, he remained with us and shared a personal moment. He gave my mum some cash for us, it was a big deal for her. She had been struggling with no help for so long it was devastating knowing her Ex-husband was out there living his life.

She appreciated his efforts and welcomed him home, except he didn't want to come home. A few hours went by, and he left, again. This time it infuriated me. "You're my dad!" I said stomping my feet in aggression. He kneeled down and patted my head "I know, just because I'm not in the house doesn't mean I'm gone. Use the landline and I'll be right here" he said. From that day I made it my mission to memorise his number, till I eventually did. I wrote it on the bunk bed to remind myself and practiced every day, remembering it became useful to me. I'd run to the landline when it rang and sit on the floor talking to him tangling the wire around my little hand. When it was bedtime, I'd call him to say goodnight and when I felt alone, I'd call him too.

CHAPTER SIX

Struggles, Bonds, and Growing Pains

My dad began making efforts to visit us again. Me, Mweeka and Benjamin enjoyed his visits, but Chimufa didn't.

Chimufa's heart began to grow cold for what my dad had done over the years, he hated his actions, and the tipping point was my dad leaving my mum. Mweeka achieved amazing results at school, so much my mum rewarded him with treats. She wanted him to become a doctor, he had the brains for it! Unfortunately, that's not what he passionately wanted to do in life. He took his own path to pursue business, but not to work in a typical office, the highest firm in the biggest cities is what he reached for! He studied almost every night and didn't miss a day of school. He made a friend called Brian, who had the same passion as him. Brian was always happy, that's the best way I can describe him, he was confident and held his head high in every room he entered.

When he would come to the house, he would treat me like his little sister and for a while I saw him like my brother. Even though my dad was back in my life, he was still distant, it was only on occasion he would drive down to Lancaster and see us, we didn't go to his place, and he didn't tell us where exactly he lived. He secretly had his own life in a different city and even got a girlfriend. We were yet to find out about her, looking back, I wish we never did! Mweeka applied for Unis, and he got accepted into his first choice, which was no surprise. We were all happy for him, he worked hard and achieved well so he deserved it. When it was my time to say goodbye as he headed off to Uni, I couldn't bare it. I needed him.

He had all the answers to my questions, who would take me to the sweets shop and let me scoff my face in chocolate. Who was going to tuck me into bed with a kiss on the forehead. Who was going to protect me. Chimufa was distant with the family, he started staying at Liam's house, Mweeka was heading off to Uni, Dad had moved to a new city, so me and Benjamin were left with Mum. We needed to stay together; it would have been for the best. Mweeka made me sweep the bedroom because it was a mess. We couldn't afford a hoover so we used a dustpan or broom. It made the job a little difficult, but it was no different to back home. He was sat in the room monitoring me and demanding I go back into the corners and get every bit of dirt. I gave him an evil stare and told him "I don't want to do this!", and without saying a word, simply raising his eyebrows made me continue. He left the room for a split second and closed the door behind him. There were sounds of people talking downstairs that I couldn't make up what they were saying.

I crawled to the door as I was already on my hands and knees and opened it slightly. "You have a new woman?" My mum yelled. I was unsure about who she was talking to, it couldn't have been my brother? "Look, you wanted a divorce" my dad replied raising his voice. My face cheered up and as I stood up to go run downstairs and greet him, I was stopped by the loudest bang. My body froze with my hands still on the door handle. "Are you okay?!" Mweeka said in panic. My dad had pushed her and as she fell backwards, she landed on the coffee table. I walked downstairs

47

slowly and watched Mweeka grab my mum's hand and help her up "I can't stand" my mum said scrunching up her face in agony. The fall backwards snapped a bone in her leg, it was traumatic to witness her in severe pain. "Dad?.." I said as I appeared at the bottom of the stairs. He looked at me, then looked at my mum and Mweeka struggling and walked out the door. I ran to the door and watched him open his car "don't come back!" I shouted with tears falling down my face.

I wanted to believe he was a good Dad, but to me, it wasn't how good he was to me, it was how he treated my mum. For the first time I had witnessed what my mum spent years dealing with, it crushed my little heart. The ambulance came to help my mum, "stay with her" she said to Mweeka. He made me finish sweeping the floor while he read his book. He looked at peace with his headphones on, as if something serious didn't just happen. As I was sweeping away, I stopped and watched him, I could feel his sad energy, something didn't feel right. Tears fell down his face and that was the first time I had ever seen him cry. I stopped what I was doing to wrap my little arms around him, he didn't tell me to get off, or pretend he was fine, that moment we shared was beautiful.

He cried silently on my little shoulder, people think men having emotions is a sign of weakness, I think the opposite. It's a sign of strength, to be in touch with how you truly feel. That one moment is what he needed, someone to cradle him and tell him it's all okay. Even though I was a child and shouldn't have been able to access that part of my brain yet, I'm glad hardship made me grow up faster, because I was able to give him that moment that he so desperately needed. After my mum was taken to hospital they put a pot on her leg, gave her crutches and she was soon back home. Benjamin returned from his friend's house, Kane. Kane's family looked after him well and treated him like their own, so my mum had a lot of trust when letting him stay over there.

Months went by and my dad was still off the radar. No calls, no visits. Mum had recovered slightly so was walking better and was able to go back to work. The period she had away from work while healing put her in a worse financial situation. The pay checks were getting shorter, and the money couldn't pay the rent. She didn't have savings, anytime she would try creating a jar of savings, she would need to dip into it to cover living expenses. Eventually we had to leave that house, it was a bitter moment because it had become home to me. Mweeka left for university, so the journey began for me, Benjamin and Mum. The sweet part about relocating homes was the fact that it was a fresh start. Our family heavily needed something new, and this house was about to be it! I was so amazed by the amount of space the garden had, and it was all to ourselves! The living room was super spacious and there was even a front garden. Me and Benjamin shared a room, and my mum got her own room.

We still kept the same bunk bed that we had since arriving in the UK, in fact we kept it for such a long time. With money falling short it was impossible getting new furniture. There was a shop in the town Centre that offered pay-as-you-go services for their furniture. When my mum had stumbled across the shop she walked right in and finally got a big TV. It was humongous, I mean, compared to the other one we had.

She surprised us with it, and we thought she was rich! We weren't aware that she couldn't afford it, but we were young and didn't care about the cost, we were just excited to have a new TV. The love we had for that TV was out of this world, we watched WWE wrestling on the TV and practice the stunts on each other even though they recommended we didn't try at home, we did anyway. It would lead to one of us getting a minor injury or one of us crying.

But we would continue it over and over again regardless! My mum wanted us to have a new happy experience, so she managed to get a few pieces of furniture from the same shop, which meant she had a lot billed to her account that she couldn't afford. The payments would often be unpaid, and she would accumulate a backlog of debt. For the sake of her kids being happy, she didn't mind. I was in my final year of primary school, but Benjamin had already started year 7 of high school. Mum picked up extra shifts and got another job at the care home for extra income. So, heading back home from school was a solo task I dreaded. I wasn't fearful of being alone, since we had moved to a different area, it was a long walking distance from the school.

There was nothing good about the area we stayed, it had a high crime rate, and the government made no efforts in taking in account how run down everything was. I slowly stopped spending time with Megan completely and even made a new friend called Teejay. She was effortlessly pretty, had long brown hair and everyone adored her, even me. She was sweet and had a lovely heart, just like me so we enjoyed each other's presence. Her mum was very welcoming, and even let me enjoy the treats she kept in her fridge.

In my early years, making friends opened my eyes to our family's financial situation. Moving to the UK from Africa was like living a dream for us. It felt like we had hit the jackpot just by being here. It was so different from the village I grew up in, and it seemed full of chances to make a better life. But here, we were seen as 'lower class.' Things I thought were great were just everyday things for others.

One day, a girl in my friend group talked about going shopping every week with her parents, picking up anything she fancied. She said it proudly, without even a hint of gratitude. She went on about how her parents kept adding £500 to her savings every week. "They've been doing it for years," she mentioned. Thinking about how much money they could set aside like that left me in awe. When she'd turn 18, she'd have this huge amount waiting for her, while I knew I'd have to start from scratch. That's the thing about not having a rich background; you don't get that initial push. With Mum working long hours, Benjamin and I often found ourselves bored at home. To kill time, we'd join the neighbourhood kids for a game of Manhunt. Here's how it worked: one person would try to tag everyone else. We'd choose that person with a quick round of rock, paper, scissors. It was simple but brought us endless joy. If they caught anyone by managing to grab them, the player who was caught joined the hunt to find the rest of the group until there was one last person to catch.

51

CHAPTER SEVEN

The Shadows of Desperation

The game had begun. As everyone scattered to find the best hiding spots, Harry, our "manhunter," covered his eyes, beginning his countdown from 10. My friends and I darted in every direction, finding refuge behind bushes, trees, and cars. Some even climbed up to the rooftops. Harry's hunt was on, and it felt like he was catching everyone. The thrill of the chase made my heart race, especially when Harry neared the spot where Benjamin and I were hiding. We could barely stifle our laughter, especially when we heard muffled giggles from the girls nearby.

"Let's get over this wall," Benjamin whispered urgently. He had spotted an escape route: a 7ft wall that opened into a back alley on the other side. Being smaller and not as strong, I needed help to get over it. Benjamin hoisted me up, and with a push, I managed to swing myself over, landing safely on the other side.

Now it was his turn. I watched as he took a few steps back, sprinted forward, and leaped, fingers grasping the wall's edge. As he prepared to swing himself over, I caught a glimpse of shattered glass below. My heart raced even faster as I shouted, "Benjamin, watch out!" But it was too late. Instead of a clean landing, he tumbled over, letting out a piercing scream as he hit the ground. Glass shards had punctured his ankle, his hands were littered with splinters, and scrapes marred his legs. My voice cracked with fear as I called out for help, trying desperately to lift him up,

trapped in the narrow alley. Blood started to pour from his ankle as he dragged his

leg and hopped on the other.

Benjamin's grip tightened around my shoulders as he tried to steady himself. With every ounce of strength I had, I supported his weight, feeling the strain on my petite frame. Meanwhile, Harry, sensing the urgency, bolted home to call for help. It wasn't long before his elder brother, like a beacon of hope, emerged from the alleyway's exit. Without a moment's hesitation, he scooped Benjamin into his arms and carried him towards safety.

 Benjamin's eyes were growing heavy, his consciousness waning, so I continuously jostled his head, urging, "Stay with me, Ben When the wail of the ambulance reached our ears, I felt a surge of hope and fear simultaneously. I found myself whispering my first ever prayer, "Hi Mr. God, please, just listen this once. Make him okay. I promise, I'll be good forever if you just make him okay," my fingers entwined tightly with his, eyes shut hard against the world. Upon our arrival at the hospital, my mum's face crumbled into anguish. She clutched him close, her voice breaking, "Why my son?" Her words were a haunting refrain. While nurses ushered me to the children's waiting area, I got wind of my father's arrival. The man we never expected to show, but he did. My mother, through her tears, seemed relieved to have him there, but anger boiled within me. "Why are you even here? You never cared!" I yelled, my feeble pushes against his chest barely making an impact. Yet, he absorbed my fury, silent and stoic.

My parents went outside of the hospital room to discuss. I wanted him to leave our family alone, but I wanted him to stay all at once. I wanted to give him just one more chance to make things right, I saw the good in him, and clung onto the good memories. After my mum spoke to him privately, they returned, my dad apologised for his actions, it sounded sincere, it sounded true.

My dad offered to drive us home to save money on a taxi, which my mum

accepted, when we got to our home, he told me to wait in the car because he needed to speak to me. We sat there for 30 minutes, I expressed my feelings, how he hurt my mum, how he hurt me. He gave his reasons, and we bonded again. In that moment my dad gave me the chance to have an open conversation with him about how I felt, that was healing to me. It opened doors for forgiveness, he was human and so was I and we all make mistakes, don't we?

Benjamin's ankle was healed, he could finally walk properly. Back to his playful self, I missed the burst of energy. My dad had got an apartment in Morecambe, the seaside town we loved to share time together at. It was perfect! He came to our house in his little blue car and told us to pack our overnight bags. My mum didn't say much, she just wished us well and told us to have a good time. They exchanged little words then we left for the weekend. The home had 2 bedrooms, there was a lovely little kitchen, dining space and a work area in the loft. "Here's your room" he said to us while opening the door. The walls were painted by him, he customised the curtains with fabric and his sawing machine. The bedding matched and were also custom made. Two single beds, one for me, one for Benjamin. "We get our own bed?!" Benjamin said running inside the room full of happiness. "Yes" my dad said proudly. He even added a desk area so I could continue my drawings in an allocated comfortable space.

The effort he taken to make us comfortable in the new home was admirable, he was really making up for his mistakes. Bike rides with the wind in my face, then stopping by the park to play were my favourite days with my dad. He had an adult bike and me and Benjamin had our kids' bike, he bought me a pink one and

54

Benjamin a blue one. Riding bikes along the promenade became our little tradition. As the waves crashed on the beach below, I pedalled forward, my helmet securely on even though I rarely ever had a mishap on the bike. Meanwhile, Benjamin was a daredevil, always attempting some bike stunt, much to our dad's dismay. "Stay safe on the road, especially when crossing!" I'd remind myself.

On Saturdays, another adventure awaited - crab fishing! We'd gather our gear, hop into the car, and drive to the special crab pond. "It's where the crabs hang out," Dad used to say. The routine was simple - catch, click a picture, and release them back.

Swimming was my passion. But life took a challenging turn, and with expenses rising and Mum's increasing work hours, I had to take a break. With Dad back, the prospect of diving back into the sport rekindled. However, the nearest available team was just too far away. So, my swimming dreams were paused, but I hoped only momentarily.

Adjusting to a new life, Dad made an effort to integrate into the English culture, often serving us traditional English dishes like sausages, mashed potatoes, and gravy. It wasn't gourmet, but as I sat at the table, my thought was, "I was just happy to eat."

One evening, as we were enjoying our meal, Dad broke the silence, "I want you to meet someone." My eyes darted to Benjamin, who seemed equally clueless. Then, in walked a lady with blonde hair. She greeted us with a smile, and Dad introduced her as 'Ann', his girlfriend. The revelation hit us hard. This wasn't our mum. And while we didn't embrace her arrival, our cold response clearly left her feeling like an outsider. I disliked her presence, she would put her hands around my dad, smile at him then smile at me. I didn't dislike her as a person, just the fact my dad chose to be with her rather than to fix things with my mum.

It made me unhappy that I had to watch someone else play the role my mum did once upon a time. Benjamin didn't mind, he was slightly older, so he knew it was for the best. He didn't want my parents to be together, he wanted my mum and dad separate. There were less arguments this way, and everyone was happy, apart from my mum. She was yet to find out about Ann, and I wish she never did for what had to come. Neither me nor Benjamin announced my father's new girlfriend to our mum. We were scared to see her reaction, instead we told Chimufa. He told my mum and he also told Mweeka over the phone. It soon became the family's hot topic, 'dad's new girlfriend'. The news about the relationship destroyed my mum, she was filled with disappointment, sadness, and jealousy. My dad treated Ann with care, patience, and understanding. He took his time with his words and actions, which he didn't do for my mum. He worshiped the ground she walked on but ruined the ground my mum walked on. He was a coward; he didn't tell my mum about Ann being in his life. My dad didn't have the decency to even let my mum know another woman would be present when we would leave for weekends.

He refused to let my mum meet Ann after countless attempts to ask, he always told her "It's none of your business". One day, I had come back from my dad's house and my mum asked me several questions about Ann. You know, it was strange. Mum suddenly started asking me questions, grown-up ones like, "Where does Ann work?" I honestly didn't have the answers and seeing her grow increasingly frustrated made me uncomfortable. "What do you do when Ann's there?" she pressed on. So, I spilled the beans. I let her in on all the moments, thinking it might ease her worry. But I could tell it wasn't the picture she had hoped to paint in her mind. She probably wished for tales of dreary weekends and monotony. But, in all honesty, I enjoyed my time at Dad's. Sure, Ann wasn't the easiest to be around, but I learned to tune her out, focusing solely on the moments with my dad.

Once I finished, Mum seemed deflated. She gave a heavy sigh and trudged to her room. As she did, this pang of regret hit me. I thought, "I should've told her that she's special too, that I cherish our time together." So, gathering my courage, I approached her door. Just before knocking, I paused. Through the door, I could hear soft sobs. It struck me then; even though Mum initiated the divorce, moving on isn't a switch you can flip. As they say, "We get accustomed to people in our lives, and when they aren't around it's like an empty space in your heart."

Dad truly missed out on a gem. Mum was one of a kind. I'd watch him, looking for something in others that only she possessed. And while people might think it's easy to forget past hurts, sometimes pain disguises itself as nostalgia. That's probably why I found Mum, curled up, shedding silent tears into her pillow. She was deserving of love and happiness, but he didn't give it to her, God has a plan for us all, and my dad was not her future, I wish she realized this sooner.

The way Chimufa was acting just seemed to spiral with each passing week. He was staying with Liam's dad, a known alcoholic. Every time you'd see the man, he'd be stumbling from one too many drinks. Chimufa found himself in a new crew: Liam and three other boys who were nothing but trouble. One of them, Ryan, had been on the streets since he was 18 after his parents, both drug addicts, left him to fend for himself. Fights became the norm for Ryan, and more often than not, Chimufa would be right there beside him. They'd duke it out on the streets until the police showed up, and then they'd take off running.

Chimufa tried to pull away from that life. "It was months since Chimufa sold weed," and after one close call with the law, he put that life behind him. He even got a job at a nearby store and seemed to be turning things around. My mum reached out to him, begging him to come back home to us, but Chimufa just wasn't having it. He loved the freedom that came with living at Liam's place. No rules, no curfews, just doing whatever he wanted.

Liam, though? He was a different story. The kid was falling apart, getting lost in the haze of weed. Every day, every hour, he was lighting up. Neglected and unloved by his own dad, he was fading away. More drugs and booze than meals and looking worse for wear. It was painful, watching him follow in his dad's footsteps. From a shy boy with so much potential, to just another lost soul.

But Chimufa? There was still something about him. He had this energy, this light. After work, he'd bike home, earphones in, rapping his heart out to Tupac. One day, though, he clocked into work and could tell right away his boss was in a foul mood. Chimufa tried to keep his head down, focusing on stacking shelves, but couldn't help overhearing his co-workers getting an earful about picking up the pace. The manager had come to his isle and demanded that Chimufa would "stop wasting time". Chimufa explained that he needed to complete stacking the shelves before starting another task so his manager walked up to his face and quietly told him "You will lose your job if you don't do as I say your black piece of shit". Chimufa looked him up and down in disgust and said "what did you just call me" while putting down the box of food. "I don't know what you're talking about you must be hearing things" the manager replied smirking. Chimufa immediately took his work badge off and threw it on the floor, walked to the staff room, put his backpack on and cycled home. He filed a complaint the next day and was fired.

The manager kept his job, and he was made jobless. He applied for new employment but was rejected each time which was disappointing for him. All he wanted to do was improve his life and work hard, but it was difficult. When Liam was smoking weed, he started to join in to calm down. The group of them started to get high at Liam's house, basting rap music on full blast, and that was his escape. He cycled around from shop to shop, to factories, and offices handing his CV, but weeks were passing, and no one had got back to him. He became so clouded with the constant smoking he forgot to check up on us like he normally did. His eyes were blood shot read, his hair was growing out, he wore the same clothes from two days ago and his shoes were battered when he opened the door.

Mum was at work like usual, so I answered and jumped on him "hey big bro" I said. "Hey little sis you're growing up" he replied while taking his shoes off. His clothes smelt bed, but I didn't want to tell him, "Have you been crying" I said looking at his eyes. "No little sis something got into my eye, so I was rubbing it" he said while tickling me. It made me emotional seeing him in that state. He hated his hair growing out, but his hair was long. He used to wear baggy T-shirts with cool prints on them and colourful shorts but now he wore black tracksuits with black trainers. The more he grew up, the more I could feel him losing himself, and I wish I could grab his hand and pull him back, but I couldn't, I was too young to help.

His job was to protect me, not the other way around. He needed someone and he had no one to talk to. My mum came home that evening tired from work and greeted him with joy after finding him asleep on the coach. She begged for him to come home but he insisted on staying with Liam. She didn't fight hard enough to keep him close because she was tired of his behaviour. But I wish she sat down with him and hugged him, told him it was all going to be okay, and he has a chance to make his life better. I wish she took the time to ask him how he was feeling and if there was anything on his mind. I always wonder if he would have turned out

60

differently if he has that person in his life. It seemed everyone who came into his life didn't care about him, pushed him to the side or wasn't a great role model. Ryan asked Chimufa to collect weed from a local dealer because he wasn't available to go collect it himself. Chimufa headed to the location on his bike and waited to spot the dealer.

A man in a black hoodie walked closer with his hands in his pockets and passed over a small black carry bag, then Chimufa handed the cash. He opened the bag and looked inside to see a vacuum-packed parcel, he pierced it open, and it was full of cocain, but he was only aware of the pouches of weed. He looked back but the man in the hoodie had already disappeared. "What is this" Chimufa said angrily passing the bag to Ryan. "Relax it's not that deep" Ryan replied while putting his bag down. "Here's your money back and some more for doing that favour for me bro" Ryan said handing over a bunch of cash. Chimufa was amazed when counting the £20 notes.

He counted £400 in cash and sat down to count it again in disbelief. He thanked his friend Ryan and proceeded to ask how he got the money. Ryan explained he had been selling drugs on the side while doing his job because his girlfriend was pregnant with his child, and they needed extra cash for their own place to stay. They were saying in accommodation provided by the council, but it was filthy, and no state for a child to grow up. He expressed that £20,000 cash was saved up from the past 7 months and he was ready to put money down for a small house in the following month in time for the new-born. Chimufa was surprised that he managed to not only save up so much but did it secretly without being caught.

He asked to be let into Ryan's money-making plan, but Ryan was greedy, he wanted all the money to himself, so he only let Chimufa have a small amount. Chimufa was tired of sitting around and getting rejected from jobs, so he started selling weed again, but this time branched out into different areas, only this time he started getting Ryan's clients. Ryan worked a job, so he wasn't actively on the streets, and people didn't enjoy waiting a specific time for his availability, so they started buying the weed from Chimufa instead. His clientele grew bigger and stronger with people coming back to him and completely not going to Ryan. Chimufa started to bring in lots of money and stuffed money in a shoe box, which was hidden in my mum's house.

He would wake up bright and early and get into his bike with his earphones, deliver drugs to people and be complete by mid-day. He was still full of energy and could go on for longer, but he didn't have enough weed, so he went behind Ryan's back and arranged a secret meeting his plug. He was able to get more than just week, but cocaine too. Chimufa made a promise to himself to acclimate enough funds to kick start his life then leave drug selling alone.

CHAPTER EIGHT

Escape and Abandonment

Everyone began to know his name in the area, he was the 'go to person' and his phone rang every other minute. He could no longer fit any more notes in the shoe box, so he got another shoe box and hid it in mum's house. When Ryan wasn't getting customers, he found out about what Chimufa was doing behind his back from word of mouth and was furious. He felt betrayed so planned on getting his revenge. Ryan made a few phone calls and went to make cash payment to someone he knew that was violent. He paid someone to do his dirty work because he didn't want to get caught while his new-born was on the way.

I remember this night clearly, it was horrific, and scarred me as a child. I had gone to bed with Benjamin sleeping below me on the bottom bunk and my mum sleeping in her room across the hallway when I heard a smash sound coming from downstairs. The window was smashed with a huge rock, breaking enough glass to allow them to jump through. They jumped through and went straight to the front room and trashed the place trying to find the boxes of money. Benjamin ran to my mum's room bravely and shook her till she woke. She quickly told him to stay quiet and get under the bed.

She tips toes to our bedroom where I was laying and told me to stay laid flat on the bed and stay quiet. She looked down the staircase and in a split second the mysterious man had run out the door and left it wide open. She called the police but didn't have much information to give them since she was clueless. It created fear in our home, the police didn't help to investigate what happened, Chimufa was still not answering his phone, so my mum was in distress. A couple days later he came back to my mum's house finding out what happened and the stress it caused my mum, so he confessed to what he was doing. My mum was unhappy with his actions, it made her feel like her job as a parent failed, she knew she tried her hardest to point him in the right direction, but I knew she questioned if she was around more, she could have prevented him turning into the boy he was.

I felt a slight sense of racism when the police questioned my mum on the event. My mum told Chimufa to leave, to pack his bags and not return, so he did exactly that. He got all his belongings in bin bags and left, I watched him walk out the door and the same sense of abandonment I felt when I watched my dad continuously leave, was the same feeling I felt in that moment. My mum decided to move house again, she said, "it isn't safe around here" and she wasn't ready to put her babies at risk.

We moved to a council estate which was worse than the other area we stayed. It was all she could afford and if it meant the same dangerous people didn't know where we lived, it was good enough. There was 3 bedrooms, a small garden wishes a shed, and a big front room. It was located near a corner store and a park around the back. A good part about the council estate was a community centre where kids could go and spend their free time to stay out of trouble. It felt as though the council build the community and dumped it there. It wasn't well kept, it had graffiti all over it, people would smoke weed on the front and take drugs around the back, rubbish was thrown everywhere, and the grass was rarely cut.

Some of the bricks were falling off, and the inside wasn't clean. It was £1 to enter the community centre, which wasn't a lot of money, so it was affordable for us. I remember my first day going alone, it was a brave move, but I built the confidence and stood there in the queue. There were kids behind me laughing, and when I turned my back they would stop, then continue when I turned away. It started making me feel uncomfortable because I was the only black child there. "You're a nigger" one of the boys said. I ignored his comment and continued to wait patiently holding onto my £1. A girl named Shannon pushed past the queue to stand behind me and said "blacks aren't allowed in here" while pulling on my hair. I quickly turned around and grabbed her hand to remove it from my Afro and told her to leave me alone.

My temper grew short the more she spoke until I finally burst when she spat in my face and called me a "paki". The ignorance was evident, she spoke derogatory terms which didn't align with my race or background. She called me "chinky smelly", almost as if the words she spoke wasn't what she knew but heard and learnt from someone else. "Do not call me that" I shouted and pushed her. She jumped on me and hit me several times around the face while I attempted to block her punches with my hands. I knew if I didn't fight back, I would end up with bruises all over my face so I kicked my legs till she wasn't on top of me no longer, hooked my legs behind hers, knocked her to the ground and kicked her in the stomach with as much force as I could.

I used the skills from my karate classes to defend myself, which became useful to me. One of the staff members came running outside and attended to Shannon laying on the floor "are you okay Shannon?" She said as she whimpered. I didn't feel bad, in fact I felt proud of myself, I gave her multiple opportunities to leave me alone, but she kept bullying me. "You need to go home!" The staff member said as she escorted me out of the line. "She was racist?" I replied while I stopped walking. I knew my rage resulted in a girl being slightly injured but I didn't like how the staff didn't care what she had done to me. I went home and explained to my mum why I didn't stay at the community centre, surprisingly she understood and hugged me tight.

Regina came over after she heard the news and gave me a pep talk about how I'm different from other people and how I should react to different scenarios. She told me the racism she experienced while being in the UK and it opened my eyes to the reality that there are multiple bad people out there. She gifted us an old computer which she saved up her money to purchase, and it was the best gift ever! The first discovery of Habbo Hotel! Which was an online computer game where you could build your own home, go to different sections of the hotel and talk among other online people. These were my favourite type of games because they were creative and interactive which was amazing for my brain.

It was the end of primary school and there was a play to finish off the school year. Everyone had selected roles and I signed up to sing on the stage. I had practiced many times at home and even practiced in front of Benjamin and my mum.

The song was called Paradise and the play was about a girl going to a magical place of happiness. I was in the school toilets when I was getting prepared to get on the stage, I was stood looking in the mirror fixing my Afro when Ellie came in. "You know you're awful at singing" she said. I turned around and said, "you know one day you will see how awful YOU are" and continued fixing my hair. She tried to put doubt in my mind before the show to throw me off, but I had great judgment of character, so I didn't allow it.

Plus, my mum promised she would leave work early come to watch me preform. It was getting closer to my time to get on the stage, and I twiddled my fingers and bit my lip. "You'll smash it" Miss.Hendrinson said handing me the mic. I walked onto the stage and the music started, the lights went down, and I could see a crowd of parents sat in their chairs filling up the room. I looked at the chair that was saved for my mum in the crowd and found it empty, I wanted to run off the stage and cry, but everyone was watching me, and I could feel their stares. I was extremely anxious walking to the centre of the stage and closed my eyes to sing. When I finished and got off the stage I ran to the changing room and collected my belongings and headed to the reception. "Is my mum here" I asked the lady at the desk. She searched the sign in sheet but didn't see my mum there, so I sat and cried. She turned up almost 30 minutes later and apologized. I didn't hate her for it, I understood that she had a responsibility, the fact she tried to come cheered me up. She took me out of school early and treated me to McDonald's and we sat and talked.

When we arrived home, Mweeka was already there. Fresh from Uni, he looked so different that it took me a moment to recognize him. Dressed in a crisp suit with neatly cut hair and the beginnings of a beard, he was a sight. Despite my game seeming of no interest to him, he gave me a warm hug and whispered, "I'm glad you're happy." That evening, it was time for my hair ritual. My mum brought out the packets of expressions, and I prepared myself for the inevitable discomfort of getting my braids done. Sitting on the floor, with my head in her lap, she would part my Afro, and I would brace myself for the tightness of each braid. Every now and then, I'd try to gauge how much was left by feeling my head, only to be swatted away by my mum with a gentle reminder to be patient. All this, in preparation for my first day in year 7 at Our Ladies Catholic School.

Our Ladies was the same school my brother Benjamin attended, and it was just a short walk from our house. Though it had a reputation for being 'religious', the uniforms were anything but modest in price. Mum, always thinking ahead, bought mine a few sizes too big to ensure they'd last. Benjamin, having already completed a year at the school, had changed. He'd become quieter and more reserved. Before my first day, he sat me down for a crash course on surviving high school. He gave advice, dos and don'ts, and made me promise to let him know if anyone troubled me. On our walk to school, he'd always be a few steps ahead, scanning for any potential issues and ensuring I made it to school safely. He didn't walk beside me, he walked in front of me, like he was on the lookout for anything dangerous. He watched the cars and made sure I crossed the roads safely and got me to school on time.

High school had a similar dynamic to primary school, except it was much bigger and scarier. The halls were long and there were lots of doors, it was confusing finding the classes alone. I was put into a Form class which was a 30 class you had to start the day, they gave you school news, updates, and you a period table that showed you what lessons you had at what time. The one thing I appreciated about high school and the system in general was the structure it gave you for your adult life, it taught you how to wake up early in the morning, plan your day ahead and know exactly what you're doing with time segments and reasonable breaks. It also taught you how to dress appropriately in a professional environment and how to get along with strangers. I thought high school would be a chance to be surrounded with people who looked like me.

Mweeka said that high school had 10x more people than primary school with different ages and different backgrounds, he made me have hope for diversity which was quite minimal at my school. I was the only black girl in the entire school which I didn't realize until a few months in. It was a nerve-racking experience to walk into the classroom and realize there was no one else black there. All the kids were forming friends and I was sat in the corner drawing in my book. The teacher noticed I was alone, came over and encouraged me to speak with the other kids. The other kids didn't want to include me in their conversations because they were talking about cool items they had.

69

Some of the girls had Hype bags, 'Jesus' bracelet, Paul's boutique bags, Nike trainers and Juicy tracksuit zip up hoodies. I didn't relate to them, I couldn't afford nice shoes, my mum purchased my shoes from shoe zone which was a store that specialised in affordable footwear. My bag was from Primark which was an affordable store for clothes, accessories, and other items. I didn't have anything fancy to show and high school kids were always trying to impress each other by what they had or what they looked like.

CHAPTER NINE

A Sister's Struggle

A few days into high school, I found myself befriending a girl named Bethany. With her long blonde hair and a put-together look, she exuded a warm presence. "You know, you're really kind," she once told me, and in that moment, I felt that our friendship would last a long time. Bethany was a beam of light during my school days. We were inseparable, catching the bus together whenever I stayed over at my dad's since she lived in Morecambe. One day, she curiously asked me, "How do you know so much about cooking and chores?" I chuckled, surprised that it was considered unusual. "Where I come from," I explained, "chores are a given. We've been cooking and cleaning since we were four!"

Meanwhile, my dear friend Benjamin had found his own circle. Although I missed our duo ruling the world, I was genuinely happy for him. And now, I had Bethany, a girl who got me like no other after years of being around boys. We bonded over shared tunes and endless conversations. As for Benjamin, he found solace in football. I would often stand by the field, rain, or shine, watching him play. Seeing him on that field, my heart swelled with pride. There was an incident with someone who was saying racial slurs to him in the field, he couldn't contain his anger, so he lashed out and beat the boy to a pulp. Everyone tried to stop him, but he kept going and going.

It was painful to watch and resulted to him being kicked off the team. He was silent that day for a while, my mom tried to speak with him and find out how he was and if he felt remorse, but he didn't. I began noticing that Benjamin was often angry. When I confided in my mum, she remarked, "It's probably from your dad's side," but that explanation did little to ease my worry. Whenever I faced tough times, Regina had been my rock, guiding and calming me. Remembering her soothing presence, I immediately called her, hoping she could talk to Benjamin. "I can't leave work early, I'll be home in 20 minutes," Regina responded, so I decided we would go to her instead.

With Benjamin in tow, I tried to keep things light, telling him, "We're just popping by Regina's for a visit." After a short 20-minute bus ride, we arrived at her cosy one-bedroom flat. Greeting us with steaming cups of coffee and a generous serving of biscuits, Regina asked, "What brings you here?" Her tone was gentle, her posture revealing a slight discomfort in her back.

I hesitated for a moment, then blurted out, "Benjamin's always so angry lately." Benjamin looked at me, seemingly taken aback that I'd shared our secret. But Regina, always the sanctuary in our lives, was the one person I trusted with this. In her comforting presence, we talked through Benjamin's emotions for about an hour. By the end of our chat, I sensed a weight had lifted off his shoulders.

As the sun set, painting a golden hue across the sky, Benjamin's infectious laughter and brilliant smile filled the air. "It's good to see him like this again," I thought. Before heading out, I couldn't help but ask Regina about Chimufa. "Oh yes," she said, "he stops by every other day on his bike, drops off the rent money, and catches up for a bit." Hearing this warmed my heart. Chimufa's spirit wasn't broken; he had just taken a few wrong turns. That didn't mean he couldn't find his way back, right?

Our evenings often revolved around the Xbox that dad had gifted us. With games like Viva Piñata, Sims, GTA, and Call of Duty, the console became a source of endless entertainment. Benjamin and I would stay up late during weekends, lost in our virtual worlds. Although we bickered over who was the better Zombies player, I held those moments close to my heart. I would often find myself wishing we could go back to those simpler days, huddled up in front of the TV.

Soon after, Chimufa returned home, vowing to turn his life around. Mum, ever the believer, trusted in his promise. Outside our home stood boxes labelled "going to Africa". Neighbours would fill them with clothes and toys, and the generosity was heart-warming. Once full, mum would send them off to Zambia, ahead of her own journey. The day she left, she planted a kiss on our foreheads and reminded us to look after the house and each other. With Mweeka off to university, it was just Chimufa, Benjamin, and me.

Upon reaching Zambia, mum distributed the collected goods to children and adults alike. But her mission didn't end there; she began constructing a school, a place to mould young minds into exceptional individuals! It was sweet watching her do this, and even though she barely gave us speeches and was always working, she remained a great role model for me. She stayed in Zambia for 4 months, but we could take care of ourselves.

Chimufa was home most of the day listening to music and writing in his book, staying out of trouble, and minding his business. The problem wasn't starting drug dealing, it was the trap. When he wanted out, and didn't want to continue doing it anymore, the person who he was selling drugs for controlled him by threatening to harm his family. I hated that he continued doing something he didn't want to do but felt like he had no choice, he was too far deep into it. It was only a month since mum left to go to Zambia and life at home was getting rocky. The electricity wasn't paid, and we started running out of food. Some days we used candles for the light and took cold showers. Mum spent all her earnings on the flight to Zambia and putting money into her new school and helping family.

She didn't have good fine decisions that left us in a hole for months. Chimufa was selling drugs again which meant he had some money together and filled the fridge up with lots of food and snacks. We don't see the issue with him selling drugs because he didn't bring it to our doorstep until one day he did or ruined everything. He was no longer selling drugs from Liam's house; he was doing it from our house.

Strangers would come in and out the house, music played till late hours of the night, and Chimufa would invite his friends to come over for drinks when we were home. I remember going downstairs for a drink of water and being yelled at to go back upstairs, I quickly ran back up the stairs and laid in bed with the covers over my head wishing mum would come back home. My mum had a close family friend which we considered as our uncle, who lives nearby. He normally came over to the house to check on us while she was away, but for the past few weeks he hadn't come over. I thought it was suspicious, so I went over and knocked on his door and waited. There was no answer, so I knocked again, opened the mailbox and shouted, "uncle are you there it's Doniwe".

I tried to open the door and to my surprise it was unlocked, I went right in, and my body froze after entering the front room. "God wouldn't allow this to happen, he wouldn't. I just know it" I thought to myself. My uncle's body hung from the ceiling soullessly and empty with a knocked over chair below him. "Help!" I yelled and yelled. The horrifying memory of realising a lovely man was gone and he had felt so much pain he took his own life scarred me. It was a sad moment in our lives, and we couldn't come to terms with it. My dad came to pick me and Benjamin up from our house and we stayed with him while my mum was away. Our family mourned my uncle's death, life had been so cruel from the earliest years of my life, but it had formed a strong character within me. My dad and Benjamin were quite alike, their temper was the same, and when in the wrong they didn't like to admit it.

They both didn't show affection too well, but one thing about Benjamin that was different was he would never hurt a woman. My brother didn't enjoy living in Morecambe with my dad, it was too far away from his friendship group, and he was getting to the age where he wanted to be outside having fun with his friends not sat at home bored. On the other hand, I enjoyed being home, I would FaceTime Bethany while I was drawing in my book or listen to music while designing something creative. Benjamin and my dad had an argument one day when Benjamin wanted to go to Lancaster to spend time with his friends, but my dad refused. He was about to put his hands on Benjamin in anger, but he stopped himself and allowed him to just leave. That day, Benjamin packed his bags and went back to my mum's house and stayed there with Chimufa. I missed him, so I asked if I could come outside with him one day with his friends and I promised to be as quiet and not get on his nerves, so he agreed.

I waited till my dad headed off to work for his night shift and then sneaked out at night-time, got on the bus with Bethany and went to Lancaster. There was a whole group of kids outside at night-time and I searched for Benjamin, I eventually found him in the crowd and hugged him. It was common all the kids in the year above would hang out at night around the park or in the town centre. This time I was there and involved, I felt cool that I was a part of the older group. "You alright Don" Adam said. Adam was one of Benjamin's close friend in the group. There were a lot of familiar faces present, I noticed them from the year above at school, some were smoking cigarettes, and some were drinking bottles of vodka.

A young boy called Fin which was my brother's close friend too was trouble. He came from money, so I didn't understand why he would be a troublemaker knowing he came from a good healthy wealthy background. We were all walking around as a group when Fin kicked a car and broke its window, the alarm burst out loud sounds and we all ran away in the same direction. Police cars were parked around the corner at night-time because the area was so problematic that they had a shift of officers ready for anything to happen every day. An officer chased us and just followed the crowd and ran. I ran as fast as I could I even lost sight of Bethany. My only thought was me and Benjamin couldn't get caught in this crowd because we were the only black people, and we'd get the blame for all the vandalism that was going on. The police caught a small group of us, some managed to escape. We were made to sit on a grass and stay still as they took the details of some girls and let them go, they put Fin in the back of the car. It was my turn to get my details taken and I smile at Benjamin, he stood up, walked over and the police officer demanded he sits back down. He was worried about what was going to happen to me, so he watched while biting his fingers nervously. "What's your name" the police officer said with one hand in his pocket, I replied and told him my name, he replied "Oh so you're Chimufa's sister, that boy is some trouble I guess the apple doesn't fall too far from the tree". It annoyed me that he attached me to my brother, it was the first time it happened but not the last. This period of my childhood was when everyone would know me as Chimufa's little sister, which wasn't great because I wasn't involved in his bad behaviour. He was friendly to everyone he met but he was a known drug dealer in the local area and soon enough the entire town. When people referred to me as his little sister, I wasn't ashamed, I enjoyed it because they knew how hardcore he was and it was almost like a threat if they tried to play with me, he's my big brother. That didn't keep me safe from all the harm I endured as a child, it only protected me for a small percentage. My dad found out about the situation with the police and scolded me for it, he threatened to "beat me", took my phone, and locked me in my room with nothing but a blank wall to stare at, I didn't make a fuss about it because it was fair, I stepped out of line, I just wish it stopped there.

The next day my dad was in a bad mood, I didn't know why but it had something to do with my brother. He was yelling on the phone at Chimufa, saying how he regrets having a son like him and some awful words. When he got off the phone I could sense his anger, it was like a vile feeling, I asked if I could go see Bethany, but he refused, I replied and said it wasn't fair I was already punished. "I'm going anyway" I said. He walked to me and grabbed me by the arm and dragged me to the bathroom. He pulled scissors from the drawers and grabbed my braids and cut them off. I begged him to stop damaging my hair, but he continued and kept going. He told me I wasn't allowed to go anywhere, and I should get back into my room. I waited till he shut his door and snuck out the house quietly and got the bus to my mum's house. When Chimufa opened the door, I hugged him and told him I never want to go back to dad's house again. I stayed at my mum's house for the following months to come alongside Benjamin.

CHAPTER TEN

The Youngest Perspective

Time was flying by, and mum still didn't make her return, the house was a mess, and the smells were foul. Chimufa was always high at this point so when I asked him for food his words were slow, and he was barely here with us. Liam came to the house along with some other young men who were swinging their jaws, had a strong stench coming from them, their hair wasn't brushed, and their pants were rolled up. I was frightened when they entered the house and dragged their feet to the front room. Benjamin was out this day with his group of friends, so I was alone at home with Chimufa. I peeped past the front room door and the young men that walked in was passed out on the sofa, so was Chimufa. There was cocaine on the table, empty beer cans, the TV was playing music and there were bags of weed and scales. I walked into the cloudy room and tugged on Chimufa's T-shirt "hey… I'm hungry" I said.

It didn't wake him up the first time, so I tried again. His eyes were bloodshot red, and he could barely understand what I was saying. He had pills in his hand and a small phone in the other. I grabbed what was in his hand and put it on the table carefully, grabbed his hand and helped him up with my little strength, walked to the kitchen guiding him and repeated myself. "I'm hungry" I said. He slurred his words and told me to order pizza using the landline phone, which is what I did. When the pizza came, I asked if he wanted some, but he passed out again, so I went upstairs and ate the pizza alone in my room.

Staring into his eyes felt soulless, it left me with an overwhelming sense of emptiness. The experience of witnessing a loved one get lost to drugs is like going through a process of mourning. The person you once knew disappears; they are no longer present, and you find yourself desperately fighting to save them. Yet, they are so deeply consumed by their addiction that rescuing them feels impossible. You hold your hand out but they're sinking endlessly. Eventually, the grief transforms into overwhelming guilt. What if I had done more? Could I have provided more assistance? As a child, I struggled to prevent losing the happy, bubbly, nerdy character of my beloved brother. It was too late and the sweet boy I grew up with was too far gone.

Bethany made me feel better when I was down, I adored her for it because if I didn't have her, I would've had nobody. When we were together, it was like a burst of electricity! Dancing like crazy in the front room, going up to random strangers and asking them if we can play on their scooter and falling off while giggling. We took goofy pictures and hopped onto the train to take us to Manchester, some days we'd spend in her room on her iPad, or we would go to KFC and eat chicken wings and sit on the rocks by the beach side. I'm glad I got to experience a friend like this, for what it was and how long it lasted it was great.

Most our lessons at school we were together, so we whispered funny things to each other, stand on the tables and mess around, push the wheelchairs across the room and get cramps from laughing too much. We even drunk alcohol for the first time together one night when we had finished school, there was a bottle of wine in my cupboard, so we took it and headed to a big field. We took turns to drink out the bottle while we sat there in our pyjamas overlooking the pretty night skies. I rolled down the hill and got mud all over my lovely pyjama bottoms and she came to pick me up laughing with the empty bottle in her hand. We stumbled our way back home with music playing loud on her phone having the best time.

I was on the phone to Mweeka crying and offloading my stress, I asked him to come home and I missed him, but he said he can't. He did show up again, but this time it was because my parents were arguing and involving him in their dispute. My dad wanted control over me, he thought my mum was a 'lost cause' and he could do a better job at raising me. I'm my mums only daughter so she refused, which caused a huge problem for my dad. My dad disrespected my mum by calling her names and he was manipulating her to believe she wasn't a good parent. When she felt damaged by his words, she called Mweeka for help "tell your dad to stop treating me this way" she said. Anytime they had a fall out about anything, Mweeka was always the person they would go take their problems to.

He was a young adult and getting his life together with his education, trying to focus on his studies but our parents were constantly involving him in their fights. He carried a lot of family weight on his back that led him to an overload of stress. One day I was at home with my mum while she showed me the pictures from her trip to Zambia, she said she met a lovely man called William and he planned to move to the

81

UK in due time. We heard a loud bang on the door and was scared to open the door, we could hear our dads voice saying, "open Elizabeth". My mum walked to the door and opened it slowly, my dad pushed the door open and said, "get her bags ready she's coming with me". He scared me when he pushed past my mum and demanded my things were packed, I didn't want to go with him I wanted to stay with my mum.

She was what I knew, who I was comfortable with, my dad had short temper and lashed out, that wasn't someone I wanted to live with. Mweeka was begging my dad to calm down and how his aggression was frightening me. I stood behind his tall slim body and held onto the bottom of his shirt and peeped over to see my mum and fed yelling at each other. I didn't understand why he was so cruel to her, and I didn't understand how she could still love him. I ran upstairs, closed my eyes, put the pillow over my head and pictured a colourful ice cream van and ordered a cone with sprinkles. I'd imagine a conversation with the man with a moustache serving me ice cream, sitting on a bench in a field full of pretty pink roses, I was at peace.

It was my coping mechanism that I used for years when I was in distress, to stop me from panicking. I grew up to hate the sounds of people yelling, I couldn't handle people raising their voice and if they did, I would put my hands over my ears, close my eyes and picture the ice cream van and a field full of roses. That coping mechanism only lasted for so long before it was no longer powerful enough to keep me from anxiety attacks. Thankfully my dad didn't win his battle at trying to take me from my mum, at least not that time. I walked to school which was just over the bridge from my mum's house in the rain. I passed myself and eventually reached school where my form teacher told me to hang my blazer to dry and why I didn't get my parents to drop me off at school. I told her my mum doesn't drive, then she asked if I could get the bus next time, I felt too embarrassed to say I couldn't afford it so I just said I will.

She didn't want me sitting in her class soaking wet so I headed to the bathroom and dried myself as much as I could with the hand dryer, went back to class and sat down. I looked at my day and the worst were to come, science. I hated my teacher, he singled me out and knew I couldn't answer the questions, then after embarrassing me he would tell me to study more. That day I had enough! "Maybe if you took extra time to help me, I would figure it out better" I said answering him back after his rude comments. He told me to get out of his class and head to Mr. Park's office who was the head of the year group. I didn't want to face what I had done so I sat in the toilets instead, a group of girls came into the bathroom gossiping about other girls in the year. I thought I was strange how they judged other people for their appearance, why didn't anyone at home teach them to be nice. I put my feet up on the toilet lid in case they bent down to see if someone was in the stall, they threw a pen in the stall that hit my head, but I stayed silent.

They finished putting their make up on and walked out, I let out a huge sigh of relief, "thank goodness" I said washing my hands and walking out. I was yet to find out, that girl was Chloe, a wretched witch I'd call her. She was evil, the biggest bully and most dangerous woman you could be friends with because she was like a snake. Our first encounter was in the dinner hall that day when she made a comment about my braids, she called them "weird" and "ugly". Bethany didn't say a word to defend

me, which I wasn't yet too bothered about, but I hoped she would come for my

defence, maybe she was scared? Chloe didn't make me scared, she irritated me,

especially when I got my food, sat down and she sat next to me to intimidate me. She

looked back at her friends sat at a different table and smiled, signaling to her friends

that she was about to do something. She knocked my drink over and it spilled on the

floor, I could no longer control my temper, so I stood up and grabbed the back of her

school shirt and dragged her back and angrily said "if you want to fight me, fight

me!".

She played the victim when the teacher came running over so they put me in

isolation and let her go freely. Isolation was where I spent most my school years, it

was a building separate from the school, torture house I called it. There were desks

split with walls, so you had nothing to look at, you had to sit there for hours, from

morning to 4pm without a break. You weren't allowed any entertainment and it was

silent. If you fell asleep, they would wake you up, and if you tried to walk out you

would be permanently expelled. I didn't deserve to spend my entire day in there, she

aggravated me! I sat there pondering around what my mum would say when they

called her and told her I was in isolation all day. I thought she would be furious, but to

my surprise when I got home, she gave me the biggest hug and asked me what

happened.

I began crying and told her a girl at school was mean to me about my braids,

she said they were beautiful, and they looked amazing on me which boosted my confidence then we enjoyed watching tennis on the TV together. Chimufa came home a few hours later and he seemed like his normal happy self, be brought chocolate for me to eat and told me to defend myself at school. "If you don't defend yourself, you will be bullied. Be tough little sis" he said sitting next to me with his arms over my shoulder. His hair was brushed this day, and had a fresh tracksuit on, he had a nice scent coming from him, but not of a male, more like a woman. I put my head on his chest and asked him why he smelt so nice, he laughed and said there's a special woman in his life. I sulked in jealousy because he didn't mean me, but he reassured me that I was the most special girl in his life.

It was a nice shock to discover someone was in his life because maybe a girl could make him better if I couldn't, so I encouraged him to pursue her. She turned out to be the worst thing he needed, she cheated on him and it left him feeling hopeless again. Imagine your spirits being lifted, sharing your memories with someone, trusting them and they betray you in such a manner. Men and women process being heartbroken differently, I believe women eat ice cream and lay in bed, order take out and watch love films while playing sad songs to induce the tears. Men on the other hand are quite hard-headed, so they tend to ignore what has happened and put their focus into a hustle or working out at the gym. It broke him to pieces and he shut himself out from the world. My 12th birthday was close, and I couldn't have been more excited, it was finally my chance to ask for a fancy bag for school, so I did. I prepared my speech and spent that day cleaning the house and being helpful to my mum. I stood by her, cleared my throat and asked for the £100 bag I had been eyeing up since school began. "Oh, I'm sorry Donnie but I won't manage" she said. "There's still a week left, maybe as a late birthday present?" I said while sitting on the edge of her bed.

The countless attempts of asking failed and my feelings were hurt. It made me feel angry towards my mum for that period, how can she work so much but still can't afford to pay for a nice gift for me, I was selfishly ignorant to the fact that there was a lot of financial responsibilities my mum had. In my eyes, me and my brothers were her only important family, so why couldn't she try help us more. But the truth is my mum's generosity has no end.

She shares her heart with many people, it's the selflessness of her that makes sure everyone is okay. She would spend her last penny on her family to make sure they were all living okay, just because she moved to the UK doesn't mean she no longer had her own brothers and sister to look out for. My mum had 8 brothers and 1 sister, her parents died (my grandparents) when she was a young girl, but her grandma (my great grandmother) was still with us. Our cousins from my mum's side were in Zambia and they were young and full of life, but couldn't afford education, so when my mum covered our expenses, she would cover theirs too one by one allowing them to attend school. When someone got sick back home, she would make sure they could get medical attention with the funds she had, and if they needed somewhere to stay, she would support with housing back home too.

She would use her last penny to help where she could, if she had money she couldn't keep it, she had to help. That was her life rule, which made things harder for us. I always found her catering for everyone else, feeding everyone, putting roofs over their heads, our entire family relied on her, but she never took a moment to care for herself. She wore plain clothes while lounging around the house, and colourful floral dresses casually. It was rare for her to go shopping for new clothes or care for the latest iPhone, in fact she remained living a simple life in order to help everyone else around her. I didn't honour her for it that day, all I cared about was myself, I was surrounded among other kids who were in a better financial situation than I was, and I was jealous that I didn't have what they did. I just wanted to fit in and not be different from the rest. When my birthday came around my mum was at work, but she came home earlier than usual, she cooked lots of food and we sat by the dinner table and ate it. She made the loveliest, warm meat pies, fresh and delicious.

Even though I didn't get a gift, I was still happy I had the time to spend with my mum. Birthdays weren't enjoyable for me, I was yet to experience one I enjoyed thoroughly, as the years went by, I started treating them like regular days to prevent the expectation of it.

CHAPTER ELEVEN

A Tale of Survival and New Beginnings

December 2013, my mum announced that we will be travelling to Zambia for a celebration of her wedding. It was abrupt, since we haven't met William before, but we supported her regardless. He seemed like a lovely man, and a chance to be with someone who truly loved and valued her. Me and Benjamin was ecstatic when we heard the news, we weren't excited for the wedding as much, more excited for the fact we could go back home. I couldn't wait for all the amazing food we were going to eat, seeing the animals, the fruits and the markets along with the music. It was about to be a reset for us after the ongoing problems we faced since arriving in the UK.

The wedding day was set to be on the 25th of December, which was unusual but unique. I stared outside of the plane window full of thrill, unable to sleep. "I can't wait to be there" I said to myself twiddling my fingers. Benjamin was asleep next to me, and my mum was on the third seat looking at photos on her phone. "This is his daughter" she said showing me a picture of a young girl on her phone. I was nervous to meet Williams kids, I knew they would be part of our family, so a good impression was needed. I couldn't pull any pranks and I had to be as nice as possible, it was a challenge I looked forward to the entire plane journey! "When are we going back to the UK" I asked my mum. "Until January" she replied. It was a good amount of time to meet our family, have the wedding, enjoy being back home, go on an adventure and then return with a clearer mind.

We stepped off the plane in Lusaka, the air was hot, as soon as I looked up in the sky, I could feel the heat of the sun radiating my face. A family friend picked us up at the airport and took us to William's house where we met the entire family. They were nice, polite and friendly, but I couldn't wait to see my cousins! We set off to my cousins home shortly after which wasn't a long drive away. My mum left me and Benjamin there meanwhile she went to see other family members since we were tired and needed to rest. Home was more comfortable for me, nobody was judged for what they didn't have, it was peaceful, and everyone happily lived no matter what they didn't have. We washed our clothes with our hands and lined them up outside on a makeshift wire that was connected block to block. We bathed with buckets, and we didn't watch TV, we spoke to one another. We cooked our food outside in a big pot, sitting on the front porch speaking with neighbours was a fun pastime.

I will never forget this day; it will live with me forever like a scar on my mind. My mum wanted us to go back to the village we were raised, so we could visit and see the family who lived there. I was more than happy to and so was Benjamin, I mean, we came all the way to Zambia so why not go back to the village. There was so much my mum had planned for our time in Zambia, so we hurried around place to place. On this day we set off to the village early, my mum put bottles of water in the car and got us seated in the back. We were having so much fun with my cousin Regina, so my mum allowed her to come with us.

Finally, we set off in the car which William was driving, down the roads for hours looking out the window looking at how beautiful Africa is, talking among each other and laughing. We had drove for 5 hours and were nearly at the village, the roads were in a really bad condition, so William stopped a few times to check the car over and when everything was clear he continued. We passed local children who were stood by the road with baskets of fruit coming up to the window to sell us some. My mum gave them cash, and they gave us fresh fruit for the journey there. It reminded me of the times I was in Zambia selling fruits and having some money to run back to the market for food.

We reached the village, and it was just as I remembered, lots of bushes, animals and a tiny community of people. There wasn't electricity at all times throughout the day, and we enjoyed being bare foot. The house was small with no bedrooms and a cone roof, somewhat like a hut. We ate freshly prepared food which was delicious, cooked beans with stew, and vegetables that were grown on the farm on land. Me, Benjamin and Regina bothered the cows that were on the land when my mum yelled at us to "leave them alone". She came over to use and explained how the locals and my family use the cows for their day-to-day life. It was interesting learning about the farm animals and their environment, when I was young, I didn't care to know, so it was nice understanding more. It made my experience back home more enjoyable. There was lots of bugs by the bushes which Benjamin picked up and chased me with, I ran and ran bare foot in the grass, and I felt so alive. I was happy for once; it was comfort, and it was home. Hours went by and it was time to set off home.

William looked exhausted so I asked my mum if it was a good idea for him to drive back from the village into the city. She expressed that he wasn't as tired as he looked, and he reassured us he was well enough to drive the distance back. The journey was almost 6 hours long, but I trusted his judgement and got into the car along with Regina and Benjamin. My mum buckled us in, and we were prepared to go. Benjamin sat behind the passenger seat by the window which was occupied by my mum, and I sat in the middle. Regina sat on the right side of me by the window, there was two empty seats behind us. The ride back home was quiet, everyone was sleepy, especially us kids. William and my mum were up talking away meanwhile Benjamin fell asleep with his head on my shoulder. Regina fell asleep next and placed her head on my other shoulder, it was comfortable until the car started to rock up and down over the bumps on the street. "It's nothing to worry about" my mum said while turning back smiling at me.

The sun had fully gone down, and it was getting dark. The roads were unclear, and it wasn't bright enough, aside from the headlights of the car you could barely see what was ahead. The roads were full of holes and rocks which made the driving experience difficult especially since there were no road lights. William drove down the road and began to slow down, he was swerving to the side and nodding his head. My mum could notice he was falling asleep so she suggested we stopped by the local town so he could get some rest for a while. We came across a gated home and buzzed the door, they welcomed us in and allowed us to freshen up and rest. We should have stayed for the night, if we did the most traumatic event would have never happened. Me, Benjamin and Regina laid peacefully on their couch together snuggled up, while my mum and William got some sleep. Only after an hour William woke to tell us he was okay and ready to continue driving.

We all got back into the car, thanked the Family and was prepared to leave until the man came running out the door to ask if he could get a lift back to the town with us. He got into the back seat which was free then we set off back onto the road. There were several bumps, and the journey was getting uncomfortable, I looked at Benjamin sleeping on the car window and couldn't believe he was asleep through all the bumps, but it made me happy he was at peace. I stroked his head and smiled, and my mum looked back to check on him. I wish it was me sat in his seat, I look back at this moment and wish I could have been the one. A few hours of driving William's head was falling, and the wheel swerved slightly until he completely fell asleep and swerved so much the car drove off the road and down the cliff side.

The car tumbled down viciously, rolling over multiple times, the windows broke, and the car was getting dented the more it went down the cliff, eventually crashing into a big tree and a puddle of water. I was upside down in my seat belt trying to open my eyes, but I couldn't. There was a shooting pain in my spine and legs. For a split moment I couldn't breathe, see, or feel nothing but excruciating pain. My mum kicked her door open while William got out his side and tried to open the back car door which was jammed. Blood was pouring everywhere and the puddle of water below the car was soon full of red, and the car was crushed. William and my mum counted "1,2,3 pull" and managed to pull the door open with their combined

92

strength. The man who joined us on the journey was heavily bleeding, but he was able to pull himself out of the car using one arm and sit on the ground.

They unbuckled my cousin Regina and pulled her out and laid her on the ground, they unbuckled me next and tried to pull me out of the car. My feet were jammed under the seats in front of me, so they were stuck, William pushed the seats while my mum carefully pulled me out the car and laid me next to Regina. "Benjamin is bleeding" I said with a broken voice and unable to see. "He's bleeding so much" I repeated. "My son!" My mum yelled while trying to unbuckle him. She managed to finally unbuckle him and could see blood pouring out of his face and mouth. My mum pulled his little body out from the car and held him in her hands, she tried to climb up the hill with him in her arms, but it was too difficult. Time was going by, and he was losing lots of blood, his body wasn't moving, and he couldn't talk. William held his hands out to help her up and she held onto Benjamin with her other hand.

William came down to help me and Regina, thankfully Regina had minor injuries, she stood up and grabbed one side of me and William grabbed the other, then they both climbed up back onto the road and sat me down. "My eyes I can't see" I repeated while crying in pain. I could sense Benjamin wasn't okay, I couldn't see him, but I could feel him losing his energy. I knew we were losing him, so I begged my mum to save him. "I can't lose my brother" I whimpered. We were on a dark road with no cars passing by no streetlights and there were no nearby stations. We were unsure where we were, and our belongings were damaged. My mum took

93

off her T-shirt and ripped it, wrapped Benjamin's head and applied pressure to reduce the bleeding.

The T-shirt was getting soaked full of his blood, and she was more fearful of his life. William stood at the road waiting for a car to pass to wave down but 10 minutes had passed and there was still no car. "We're going to have to walk to the nearest town" he said. "My son has lost consciousness" my mum said crying while holding him in her arms. William came to me to help me up, but I couldn't stand on my feet. "I. Can't stand" I said fearfully. "There's glass in your eyes we need to take it out" William said as he looked at my face. Regina removed her top and gave it to William, he carefully picked the pieces of glass from my eyes. My vision was blurry, but I could make up what I could see. Headlights were shining from the distance, so William quickly waved his hands, as the lights came closer the car slowed down. It was a car with a flat bed at the back and the man nicely helped us up.

When he was driving, I could feel the sadness coming from my mum. She prayed repeatedly and cried for her son. I was scared to lose my brother, he was too young, and he was my best friend, I refused to live my life without him, so I prayed too. We all did. His little body was laying in my mums' arms slowly leaving us. After driving for 20 minutes, we finally reached a hospital. We rushed in and got medical attention after my mum yelled at the desk to do something. They laid me down and wheeled me to a different room from my brother. "I need to be with him!" I shouted in frustration. I tried to get up, but the nurses pinned me to the bed. "Please let me be with him" I cried to her. "Close your eyes you will damage them" she said with her arms on my chest to prevent me from getting up. I laid in the hospital bed in pain, the sensation from my legs were gone and I couldn't feel my feet. I looked down at my feet and they were covered in blood. "My feet, what has happened to my feet" I said to the nurse in tears.

There wasn't a lot of doctors working in the hospital and they all attended to Benjamin who had severe injuries. "A doctor will be here soon, stay calm and keep your eyes shut, don't worry" the nurse replied. I put my head back and shut my eyes. Nobody can prepare you for such life events, they just come at you and in an instance, you're just figuring out how to get through it, you don't know how but you believe everything will be okay, that's what you call faith. I was uncertain about God, I had belief that he was real, but not until that moment. I finally believed in him, it took a long time to fully understand the purpose of him, he was there to help me in times where I didn't know what to do and who to turn to. The thing about faith is, you cling onto it when you need it most. I was alone with the nurse in that room all alone and all I had was faith to get me by, I was in discomfort and ache and the only thing that stopped my panic was believing it will all be okay.

My mum used the hospital phone to call my dad, luckily, he answered. He was stressed and didn't know what to do while he was in another country and his two kids were involved in a car accident. My dad told my mum that we need to fly to the UK so a doctor can attend to us there because he believed in Zambia a lot of the doctors wouldn't have been able to fix us properly. There are some amazing doctors, but the hospital we were at didn't have the best care, but it was nearby so we had to

95

undergo the surgery. My brother was first, he needed immediate attention, his life was on a thin string and his body couldn't last the 8-hour flight it would have taken to go to the UK. My dad was willing to pay anything to get onto an airplane ambulance, he would have gone into debt if he needed to, but the time Benjamin had been enough. The operation started and Benjamin slowly woke and gained consciousness. I heard his loud screams from the other room, it was an intense and brutal experience. Sitting through it made me ball in tears, he didn't deserve this treatment, he deserved better. Because he laid his head on the window, during the car crash the glass and pressure has split the front of his forehead open.

The cut was deep and severe and went from the top of his head all the way down to the centre of his eyes. Both his eyes were extremely swollen, bruised, and cuts were all over his face. He had fractures all over his little body and he sustained some swelling on his upper body. "He has lost a lot of blood, but we are doing everything we can to help your son" the doctor said to my mum. The doctors attended me next, starting with my eyes, I had minor cuts around my eyes, tiny, shattered glass entered my eyes preventing me from opening them properly, they removed all the pieces, and worked on my legs. I have 16 cuts on my legs and 4 were big and deep, my right foot was completely swollen and bruised, and my left foot was fractured. The toes on my left foot were broken into pieces and shifted place. My tiny feet were crushed with the seats in front, and glass parts pierced through skin on my leg. They gave me medicine to reduce the pain then operated on my feet. The medicine wasn't strong enough, but the swelling resulted to me feeling little pain.

When they were done, they put my bed next to my brother and I held his hand, "you'll be okay" I whimpered. The hospital was packed of sick and injured patients, mourning families and broken hearts, it was cruel and heart-breaking. The man who joined us was seen by doctors who did their best to save his arm which was half cut open. His family came to see him, I couldn't stop thinking how much sadness he felt. One decision affected all our lives, but that's the sad reality about life, we just don't know what's next. My mum and William had airbags to save them from any major injuries, although my mum had grazed her entire front chest. Regina was bruised, but she was okay, it made me relieved that she wasn't incredibly hurt. We stayed at the hospital for a few weeks, Benjamin needed constant medical attention, but I was able to keep my eyes open without pain and they put a cast on my legs allowing me to be discharged.

My mum took me back to my uncle's house where I rested in bed wishing my brother a safe recovery. My mum travelled back to the hospital, and he could finally open his eyes and talk, but he spoke slowly and quietly. She took him to the bathroom and told him not to look in the mirror, he did anyway and stood there still staring at his reflection. He was devastated by what he seen, his face was different and frightened him. He could barely recall the events of the accident, he experienced trauma from it. He was lucky to be alive, the injury should have killed him, but it didn't thankfully, he was happy to be alive and well and spent the next few days recovering.

97

While I was at my uncle's home I refused to eat, my spirits were low, and my appetite was gone. My body was in so much agony I didn't realize I was bitten by mosquitoes several times which led to me being very sick. I could barely walk and needed assistance going to the bathroom which I did often.

I was vomiting and having diarrhoea, my temperature was very high at times and was incredibly nauseous. I became bed bound because of my stomach pains, but my great grandma looked after me well. She had a hot bucket of water by my bed and wiped my body down from my heavy sweats, she changed my clothes, and she gave me soup. My brother soon joined me at my uncle's home and needed to stay in bed too, but he was in pain from the accident injury. They stitched his head together that was cut open, but the swelling hadn't yet fully gone down. The doctors did their best, but the surgery wasn't done the best. If he had undergone surgery in the UK or a better hospital, he would have had better work done. My mums wedding was getting closer, and it was about to start in a few days. We were both not fully healed but I recovered enough to stand and walk alone.

Benjamin was able to stay up for a short time, but he wasn't in the best condition, so he rested for longer. Mweeka heard about the news, and we were able to speak to him over the phone, Chimufa heard too, and we spoke. I missed them both so much and wished they could be there for us, but they were in the UK, so they comforted me and Benjamin while on the call. "I can't live my life without you" I said to Benjamin. "I'm not going anywhere" he replied while smiling. We hugged each other and spent the day in the garden soaking in some sun with Regina. Regina was young and was a few years below us, she was named after Grandma Regina in the UK which was nice because when she was around it reminded me of her. My mum had left to go to a kitchen party which was a traditional celebration for the wedding. She was still preparing for the wedding; it was going ahead as planned but I dreaded to go. When the time came around, I had to walk with crutches, my dress had to be changed too since I had a cast on my leg.

Benjamin was present at the wedding, and I was so proud of him for being strong enough to attend. We only stayed for the ceremony but didn't stay for the after party. The whole experience of going through the car crash, then the recovery process, while getting sick was overwhelming, it was stressful, and traumatizing. The injuries from the car crash resulted in scars all over my leg and my toes not properly healing due to the poor medical attention. Benjamin's scar was visible because of the poor medical attention too, but we were both so grateful to be alive, that's what mattered. My mum was married to William, and he was officially a part of our family, even though we had a huge accident, it was still a new beginning for her.

CHAPTER TWELVE

Family, Struggles, and Resilience

When we were on the bus going through Lusaka, there was a big bus crash a few cars in front of us which was fatal. We all had to get off the bus and walk, when we walked past the crash the bus was crushed at the front, there was body parts beside it, people's bodies were covered in blood, and I couldn't stop looking despite being told not to look. It was so hard to see so many lives lost. It traumatized me, that's when the car crash flashbacks started. I stood with my eyes closed and my hands over my ears blocking out the painful screams. Witnessing things like this at an early age was tough, it painted bad marks on my memories that were too hard to erase.

We ended up staying in Zambia to recover and spend more time with family for 5 whole months more. Things back home were getting bad, Chimufa was selling drugs to a wider scale of people and Mweeka was out parting with his friends at university constantly getting drunk. Mweeka still studied hard and didn't let his fun get in the way of his education, but the party lifestyle was catching up to him. He was having multiple love interests which was causing problems and strains, with petty arguments one of which resulted to an injury. He had put his hand inside the car door while it was open, and a girl slammed it shut and broke his fingers. He had the right medical attention, but he needed mum to be around during this time, but she wasn't.

Chimufa needed mum to be around to encourage him to make better decisions, but she wasn't. They were both growing into adults but needed the right guidance and role model near them, but they had to rely on themselves. The day we came back to the UK was awful, the transition of the weather was unbearable. We arrived a day early than announced to Chimufa, so he didn't get the heads up to sort and arrange the house back in order. My mum came home to everything a mess, it was filthy, and drugs and alcohol were everywhere, they had a huge fight and Chimufa left. I ran outside and begged him to stay and not to go but he refused. "I can't be here forever remembering little sis you got this" he said. Mweeka was always at parties any chance he could get, indulging in alcohol, he started avoiding family problems as much as he could. So much we don't even know he had an accident until he was fully recovered.

My dad came to visit and was in shock to see the results of the doctor's work. "I knew they should have got treatment in the UK" he said to my mum while looking at us in detail. "Don't make that face" I said pushing him away from Benjamin. I hated how he screwed his face when looking at his scar, it was damaging to his confidence. That's not what he needed to hear, he needed comfort and support. I grabbed Benjamin's hand and walked away from my dad. "Is it that bad" he said, "no he's over exaggerating" I replied.

It was time to go back to school after they was prepared to file a complaint about my absence and permanently kick me out, my mum had received a fine too. I was nervous because my cast was still on, mum hadn't made an appointment yet since she hurried back to work, and Benjamin was worried about people at school seeing his scar. I tried to reassure him as much as I could and prepare him, but he didn't need much of a confidence boost because the reaction from school didn't go as we thought.

When we got to school, we were welcomed by everyone in class and the teachers, it was like a happy celebration. All the kids were dying to hear more about the accident and how we miraculously survived. They crowded around me and said they are happy I'm doing well, and they did the same to my brother.

It was a lovely moment for me, I was invisible, unheard, until that day. The entire school knew our names and that we had a tragic car accident while on holiday. The word had got round in our town, so everyone was talking about it among each other, and I was able to share the story. People didn't look at Benjamin any different for his scars on his face, they admired him and thought it was cool. They knew how brave he was for experiencing such a horrible crash, undergoing surgery and coming out laughing and smiling.

In my culture when a girl gets her period it's a sign that she is entering puberty and the adult ladies of the close family come together to teach her about womanhood. It's a beautiful thing and experience that allowed me to learn a lot about my body. My aunties came to have a conversation with me that was gentle and sweet. They taught me about mood swings, how to handle my emotions, how to stay clean and options for periods. I'm glad I had this support because I always felt shy to talk to my mum about this subject. I always wonder what support my brothers had or if they even had any. Chimufa was still refusing to speak to my dad, they had gone

such a long time without properly communicating. My dad was brutal to Chimufa, he

was very angry about his life decisions which was understandable but the horrible

words he would say to him broke my heart. He would yell and scream in his face, tell

him he was useless, and that his future was doomed.

He fed him negative thoughts and broke him into pieces by saying things like

he didn't want anything to do with him, he's an excuse of a son and he's clueless.

African households can be tough, some families are easier going and you'd be lucky

if that was the case for you. It's rare for an African dad to show empathy and emotion

towards their child, they set a goal for their child and if the child doesn't meet their

expectations, they're considered a failure. The harsh treatment only made Chimufa

even worse, what if my dad sat him down and provided him different options or

helped him find a way out. Chimufa became trapped with selling drugs way more

than he was trapped before, he was on the police radar, he was getting in knife fights

over drugs, running from the police, he was so far in, how could he go back? No

matter how much I tried to plead him to move to a different city with a new name and

start over, he didn't want to listen to me. He told me wherever he goes they would

find him anyway, and there was no getting out.

I was at home alone one day and I could hear screaming coming from outside,

there was men shouting on the street but when I jumped out of bed and looked

outside the window through the gap of my curtains I could barely see. It was too dark

outside, so I ran downstairs, open the door and peeped out to see Chimufa and 3 men bothering him. There was a group of girls standing around yelling "leave him alone". I couldn't make out what was happening, I ran inside, grabbed my phone and called Benjamin "come home please something is going on with Chimufa" I said panicking. He hung up the phone after letting me know he's going to head back with his friends as soon as possible. When I got off the phone and looked outside, I couldn't see anyone there, I was scared and didn't know what to do, I couldn't just sit back and wait for my brother, so I went to my room and threw on some clothes. I put on a hoodie, joggers and my trainers, grabbed my phone and ran outside of the door, I didn't know what direction to run but I noticed one of the girls who was stood outside earlier was there crying talking on the phone. I ran up to her and said, "excuse me what happened, and where did they go?", "three men were trying to stab a guy, they went that way" she pointed to the direction. I thanked her and ran to the direction she pointed. It turned out the girl I spoke to on the street was trying to prevent a young man and his friends from hurting my brother. They attempted to rob him but failed when he wasn't intimidated, so they pulled out a knife on him to try stab him, he defended himself by knocking a knife out of one man's hand and fighting off the other, it got heated so he ran. While I was running towards their direction, Benjamin passed me on his bike with his friends "follow me!" I yelled, they stopped and turned around and biked ahead of me. Adrenalin was pumping through my body; I was running really fast, but I wasn't getting tired of losing my breath. I caught up to them to find Chimufa lying on the ground covered in blood and Benjamin holding down on his stomach. I was frightened and scared, I kneeled down and put my fingers on his neck to feel for a heartbeat. Thankfully he was still alive, the ambulance came very quick and took him to the hospital. I couldn't believe something like this could happen, that was the final straw for me. I went to visit Regina and begged her to speak with Chimufa, he wouldn't listen to anyone else, and he desperately needed to move to a new city.

She visited him in hospital and spoke with him, their conversation was long and deep, I didn't ever see my brother shed a tear, but with Regina he would. She told me he hoped to change his life around and wants to make the effort to do so, he had plans to get a job in construction if they would allow him. He said he would stop smoking weed and taking drugs and change his life around, it made me so happy. The beauty in life is that no matter if you fall and stumble on the way, you still have a chance at the fruitful life you once dreamed of. Those who were lost can still be found again and he was on his journey to find himself. A moving van came to the house one day which was odd, we weren't expecting a moving van of which I knew, and only Benjamin was home. The man knocked on the door then proceeded to offload furniture which looked exactly like my granny Regina's. Regina appeared and looked different; it was a few months since I last seen her but not a long time that would make someone look as significantly different as she did. She wore a scarf and a big coat to her feet with gloves as if it was the coldest day of winter. Her face was pale and skinny, and she walked carefully. "Hello baby" she said while opening her arms welcoming my hug. She had moved into my mum's house, which was bizarre, why would she do that? I could sense her tiredness when she sat on her sofa which was moved into our front room. She fell asleep so I put a blanket over her and allowed her to rest.

When my mum came home, she was exhausted from work, put her bags down and let out a big sigh, I headed to the kitchen to make her some food. "What do you want to eat mum?" I said looking in the cupboards. There was nothing but half a loaf of bread, some seasoning and noodles. I opened her fridge and there were eggs which was great because she loved eggs. I made Nshima with eggs for her. I took it to her in the front room with a bowl of water to wash her hands. She washed her hands and ate then fell asleep on the sofa beside granny Regina. They both slept in the front room that day which was really cute. I felt as if something was wrong with Regina, when mum came home, I was an extremely observant child and even more as I grew. When my mum came home, she wasn't shocked to find Regina there, not even the fact all her belongings were there. She didn't ask any questions either, it was like she already knew. She looked at Regina sleeping on the chair but didn't comment on the fact she looked so frail and worn out. I did the laundry and dishes, cleaned the rooms and sat down to draw when I was done. It was common that I would take care of the house, my mum trained me how to cook and clean for an entire household. It was respectable for a woman to know how to do these tasks especially in my culture. It taught me responsibility, organisation and discipline learning this from a child. A lot of parents choose to 'baby' their kids by doing everything for them, but they go out into the world not knowing how to help themselves with preparing meals and keeping their environment tidy.

CHAPTER THIRTEEN

Scars of Survival

The weight of the world felt heavy, pressing down upon me. There's a peculiar kind of pain that is born from betrayal, especially when it stems from someone you once trusted. This was a dark moment in my childhood, I was so young, but my trust was violated. It started like any other day. The sun was out, and everyone was waking up. But in the depths of that ordinary day, something dark was brewing. My brother had a childhood friend that would visit quite often. Sometimes, I'd join him, and we would all sit and play games in their room. His friend had quite a big family, and the siblings were all quite close in age. Their family dynamic was broken, no better than mine. I guess that's why we related to them. There was no bedtime in their household, they went to sleep whenever they wished! One of the brothers argued back with their parents but they would allow it, not punish him, just ignore him. His behaviour was awful and hard to tolerate while being around him. He was notorious for being mischievous, stealing from shops, disrespecting teachers, foul language and was always naughty. His brother was quiet, loved books, sat in the corner peacefully learning about animals and new discoveries. Their parents didn't work, they had no job and spent most their days sat on the front garden with a cigarette in their hands talking to neighbours or drunk passed out on the sofa. They didn't cook, ever. Instead, they would get in the car, head to the chip shop and come back with a small portion of chips to share over their 3 kids. Me and my brother didn't eat there, my mom told me it was forbidden for us to eat at other people's houses, I guess she was just looking out for us. I'd go over there some days on my own when I was bored at home and wanted someone to play with. Nathan's mum was smoking weed when I knocked on the door, she stepped aside, and I walked in. I found Nathan playing games on his own in the front room and sat down with him. We chatted for a while until I heard strange sounds coming from upstairs, it was as if someone was banging on the walls. "They're having sex, they do it all the time." He said looking at me then continuing to play on his game. I tried to ignore it, but it made me uncomfortable, so I asked if he wanted to play at the park which he agreed to. We played at the park for a few hours which was fun, but it was getting late, and I needed to head back home. On the way back Nathan wanted to see his brother Cameron, but I didn't have enough time, so I told him I'd head home. Nathan's Dad promised to take me home that day, so I went back to Nathan's house, knocked on the door then waited. His dad was stood there in shorts and a shirt that looked like it hadn't been washed for days. "Please can you take me home." I said smiling. He asked me to wait on the sofa while he gets his shoes on, so I walked in and took a seat. It was awfully quiet, no one was at home, Nathan's Mom had left to go somewhere because her car wasn't parked outside. His Dad was taking a while upstairs, I didn't question it, I just swung my feet and waited patiently. He eventually came down the stairs, with no shoes on, locked the door and walked over to me. My heart was racing, I immediately felt uncomfortable and uncertain of what was about to happen. He was someone I had known for a while; I could trust him… Right? Well, more like an acquaintance that

I had casual conversations with when I was hanging out with his son. Without waiting

for a nod of agreement or even a hint of consent, he forced me into a situation I

hadn't anticipated.

He shut the curtains then I quickly stood up. Before I knew it, he hit me so hard

around the face then grabbed my little arm. I tried to scream and tell him to get off

me, but it wasn't enough. He was big in size, heavy in weight and tall, I couldn't stand

a chance. He dragged me upstairs and threw me on his bed that was unmade from

the sex he had just finished with his intoxicated girlfriend. He slammed the door shut

and walked closer to me, I tried to get off the bed while maintaining eye contact. I

looked at the closed door to notice a tripod and camera set up in the corner of the

room. "What are you doing? What are you doing?" I shouted. I started screaming

"Help!" as loud as I could, my voice began to break I was screaming so much. I

managed to get off the bed and was stood on the opposite side, I calculated in my

head that if I could quickly run to the door before he tries to stop me, I could get out

of the house. I slowly shuffled, then pounced at the door, but it was locked, I twisted

the lock, but it delayed my time to escape the room. He grabbed my arm and threw

me back on the bed then began undressing himself. The worst part about this

experience was he didn't say a word, he just stared at my little body, licking his lips

and lifting his eyebrows. I turned my head to check the window, I knew I could jump

out if I had enough time to open it. I knew I could make the jump because there was

a roof below that Cameron always mischievously jumped on. While he was

109

unbuttoning his blue shirt, I quickly got to the window, opened it and climbed out as fast as I could, he grabbed my t-shirt from behind to pull me back in, but he lost grip, so I jumped on the bottom roof, then jumped to the grass. I climbed over the gate and ran, I had no thoughts running through my mind, I just ran. The violation was a lot to process, it was a horror, cold and calculated move.

For days, I was stuck with shock, anger, and profound sadness. The tape replayed in my mind over and over, each time engraving the traumatic episode deeper into my mind. What would have happened to me, what if I didn't escape? I asked myself questions but found no peace in the answers. I had been taken advantage of, from someone I was supposed to trust, it hurt me. I didn't speak of what happened that day, I stayed silent, I just promised myself to never see Nathan or his family again. I knew he wasn't to blame for his wicked Dad, I was too scared to face him and look at him in the face that resembled his dad knowing the trauma he put me through. was not just a violation of my privacy—it was a ruthless invasion of my soul.

The path of healing is long and winding, filled with moments of despair, anger, and eventual acceptance. The pain lingers, but with time, it fades into the background, overshadowed by the love, understanding, and support of those who truly matter. This chapter of my life serves as a stark reminder of the fragility of trust and the profound strength that emerges from adversity.

Being 13 years old was a time of my life I won't forget, I was outgoing, adventurous and brave. When it was summer, everyone would head to the lakes. It was a beautiful big lake which had lots of trees and nature. There would be a planned day and time where everyone would be going to the Jetty, we would pack our bags full of pop and alcohol, some people brought food, and someone would bring a speaker. Everyone would set off walking but there would be others who joined late so would walk in their own friendship group behind. Music was blaring out the speaker as we all walked down the pathway which was a 20-minute walk. We were in a group of 40 plus people. Everyone was from different schools and different years which made it fun. Beth and I were together, she had a bag which had Vodka and a Coca Cola bottle inside. I wore my bikini under my clothes and so did she.

The songs of that year were nostalgic, they played for years to come and was a staple in our generation. The playlist included "Rae Sremmurd - no type", "Dej Loaf - try me", "Young thug & Rich Homie Quan - Lifestyle", "Migo's - fight night" and more! When we reached the Jetty, the water was still, and the sun was beaming, everyone was talking and laughing and the music was good, it was incredibly good vibes. There was a huge bridge which was extremely high that went over the river, I took my T-shirt off by the bush and left my shorts on, Beth did the same and we had a drink of our liquor. There was a lot of people I didn't know who was there, so we felt a bit shy but after having some drinks and listening to music we were more relaxed. Some girls were sunbathing on the wood side, and the boys were jumping off the jetty into the water, climbing up and then doing different tricks while jumping off.

111

Plastic cups were handed around and everyone poured their drinks and we enjoyed drinks while dancing. There were people smoking weed and some smoking cigarettes while talking to each other laughing away. A boy shouted, "watch me jump off that bridge" and pointed towards the big bridge. Everyone gasped and cheered him on, he ran to the bridge, walked up the stairs and got onto the bridge. He climbed over the rail and stood there for a split moment and yelled "let's goooo!". Everyone had their phones out recording him as he jumped off the bridge and landed in the water. When his body hit the water, it was a huge splash, for a moment we didn't see him come up but then he did! We all cheered, clapped and laughed; it was amazing. These were the summers that mattered to me, I could forget about home and the trouble that was going on, I could be free and figure life out.

On the walk back there was a group of boys who were two years above me that walked by. They were talking loudly and stopped to say hello to Beth. It was really cool for someone in the years above to recognize us, so I was so excited for her. I noticed a boy with his hands in his pockets who didn't talk, I couldn't work him out, I didn't know if he was shy or too cool to speak to us. He started play fighting with his friend and I realized he wasn't shy; he just didn't notice me. I froze when our eyes locked, he was so handsome, his hair was brown and he was really tall, he smiled, and they continued walking. I was dying to know who he was, and if I could ever see him again. Beth told me his name, Ross Mayers.

I hadn't made a black friend and I felt so different to everyone else. I wanted to fit in so I would straighten my hair, but when it wasn't straight for a long period of time I would buy a box of relaxer, go to the bathroom and relax my hair. Relaxer is a chemical that burns your Afro to keep it permanently straight. It ruins your hair and damages it but when you're as desperate as I was, that didn't matter. Lauren was the sister of Chloe, who was nicer to me when she wanted to be, but this day she decided to do something horrible. She made a post about me on Facebook which said I was 'ugly', people found it amusing and teased me under the post, it was getting out of control to the point there was hundreds of comments. They attacked me for my facial features, my hair, how I dressed, my race and more.

Beth told me to check my phone and when I came across the post, I sat there reading comments crying my eyes out. I didn't do anything to these people so why would they be so hateful towards me. I wasn't going to allow people to belittle me when my brothers taught me better, so I wiped my tears and started attacking people back in the comments. There were strangers who backed me in the comments, responding to the hateful comments of the bitter girls telling them to leave me alone. Eventually the love overpowered the hate, but I didn't see Beth comment anything to them to defend me. It hurt my feelings that my best friend didn't defend me in a moment I needed her most. When I confronted her about it, she said she didn't want to get involved, even though it hurt I understood. She was quiet and the bullies would have picked on her too, so I didn't want her to experience it, so I understood.

The following day when I went to school I had IT, which was a tech class we all had to take. Beth wasn't in my class which I dreaded because the classes without her were so long and boring. I sat by my computer getting on with the task when I heard some giggles behind me, I turned around to see Chelsey laughing with scissors in one hand and my braids cut off in her other hand. She threw it on the floor, and I quickly ran to the bathroom to check my hair. It was a mess. I was lost for words and upset. My mum spent hours doing my hair just for someone to cut it off at school. I was fed up, broken and tired. Why don't the other kids in the class stop her? Why didn't anyone jump to my defence? I questioned myself and the more I did, the more it made me feel so alone.

When I told Beth she was so shocked it happened, but she couldn't relate, being a white girl in my school was easy, you could focus on your education without constantly having to deal with the racism or discrimination, I wished I could have had that. When your sad emotions get the better of you, you lose yourself. You have no control over what you do it's almost as if depression takes the lead. I was so sunken with sadness it felt like shadows were haunting me, giving me nightmares and anxiety when I tried to sleep. The stress and overload were piling on top of me like hundreds of people weighing themselves down. I looked in the mirror that night I got home with my eyes red and sore from crying most the day. "I hate you" I said with my voice breaking. It wasn't enough. "I hate you!" I shouted and punched the mirror at the disgust of my own reflection.

I was so broken inside, and I was begging for someone to help me, anyone. My offloading anger didn't help me feel any better, so I resulted in a painful act to hurt myself. Maybe if I had hurt myself, I would have got what I deserved, nothing but pain. Life gave me so much pain I was beginning to believe it was what I deserved. I broke the pencil sharpener that was in my school back, sat on the floor with the blade in my hand and closed my eyes. When the blade pierced my skin for the very first time it was satisfying, but painful. "I hate you" I whispered quietly while digging the blade through the skin on my arms and blood gushing out. I didn't know when to stop, the more I kept going the better it relieved me. The more painful it was, the more I felt so out of the world and loss of touch to my own body. Pain changes you; it makes you do things you would have never imagined before.

I laid on my bed crying with an old T-shirt I found in my bedroom corner wrapped around my arm. "I don't want to be here" I said putting a pillow over myself to block out the white noise. I was laid in silence with nothing but my thoughts. I woke up the following day as if nothing happened, I got myself prepared for school and got into class on time. Thankfully my uniform had long sleeves so I could cover the mess I made of my arm that night. I held my arm in class feeling pain from my self-harm, I couldn't hide the fact it was uncomfortable, so I rushed to the toilet to check. I hated what I seen, it was a reminder of the shallow state I was in, a reminder that things are still not okay no matter how much I wanted to pretend that morning, that was my reminder. My teacher was suspicious from blood marks on the sleeves of my light blue shirt. She waited till class ended and asked me to roll my sleeves up. "Did you do this?" She asked me in an empty room with just her and I. "Yes" I replied looking at the ground.

I was ashamed, I didn't want her to think I was weak, I didn't want to talk about why I did what I did. "It was an accident" I quickly said. I grabbed my bag and ran out the room, down the hallway and outside. I kept my problems to myself to prevent being a burden on other people's lives. My mum had a close friend who just gave birth to her child. The baby was beautiful, big brown eyes and the curliest hair. She was struggling to work while taking care of her new-born baby, so I volunteered to step in and help babysit. It would only be a few days, but it was great to earn extra cash. Taking care of a child was a breeze, I loved them like they were my own.

Being from Africa it's common for girls to be leaders of a household, this would mean the cleaning and care of people in the home, so it was familiar to me. I had a routine of everything I needed to get done for Counsel, such as when her bottle was ready and when she would typically nap. Her cries were loud and hurt my ears, but I didn't find it difficult to put her down for her sleep. I'd head to school the following day with barely any rest but happy I had extra money for the cafeteria. The food available was glorious to me, they laid it out and a different dish would be present every day!

Everyone at school hated the food, they said it wasn't nice or tasty, they complained a lot and a lot of them through most of it away. What a waste, I would think to myself after watching people take one bite and be done with their meal, I ate everything. Some days I'd know food won't be at home, so it was my chance to eat up. I'd only have £10 for the hours of babysitting I did the following evening so half would have been gone by the end of the school day. I was still grateful because my mum had gone a few days without money. I valued every penny I had in my pocket, and every meal I had in my stomach, there was no option whether I liked the food, I just had to eat. There was no option for how much I got paid, I just had to receive. My early years in life was survival mode, what's next, what more can I do, how can I make the most out of this. I found myself questioning myself every day, my brain never rested from all the worries I had.

William remained in Zambia when we returned, his visa wasn't prepared yet, but my mum was excited to have him with us. I resented him for the car accident, how could he be so irresponsible, it almost cost us our life and we had scars that lived with us forever. Any time I would hear his name it would drag me back to the moment I witnessed his head sway from falling asleep at the wheel. "Look at my toes" I said to my mum lifting my feet. "Wow, they're healing" she said rubbing them. She was trying to make me feel better, but I knew they looked different to the other foot. When my toes were broken, they weren't fixed properly by the doctor. They healed in a slightly off angle, and some of them were so crushed that they healed together. A lot of sensation was lost in my toes that ruined my balance when I walked for a long time, and I could no longer wiggle my toes around. William was due to fly to the UK in a few weeks and I wasn't looking forward to it.

Of course, I wanted my mum to be happy but with that guy? He wasn't good for her, he was careless and had no sympathy, I could feel his energy from a mile

117

away. They say trust your kids for a reason, my mum didn't trust my judgment. If she did, it could have saved her from the pain he was about to bring upon her. My mum discovered William had a second wife and lied to her throughout their relationship. He persuaded her to have the marriage so quickly so he could obtain a visa and relocate to the UK. He used her for his own benefit, knowing how much of a lovely woman she was, it was a perfect target for him.

CHAPTER FOURTEEN

A lot of people in Africa are so desperate to get out, they believe there's a bigger, better world out here than the motherland. Some would do anything to get a chance to live the life of the western world. My mum was unfortunately the victim of one of their wrongful desperate attempts. She was crying in her room, with the door shut, her phone was off, and we were worried for her. Benjamin called Mweeka to come instantly to help her deal with the news, and he did. He came and dropped his bags downstairs, walked up to her door and knocked gently, when he walked in, he found her laying on her bed drowning in her tears, so he hugged her. He comforted her but she couldn't seem to settle. "I'm going to kill myself no one loves me" she said repeatedly.

I sat on the stairs overhearing her with my heart broken. "I love her" I said to myself. I couldn't feel her pain through her voice, it felt so raw and so real when she spoke those words. I began imagining my life without my mum and the horrific experience it would be to say my last goodbyes to her. 30 minutes later Mweeka was sat by her door wide awake. I crawled up the stairs and asked what was going on. He said he'll explain in the morning and that I need to get rest for school. When I woke up, he was still sat there, wide awake. "Did you sleep" I asked him while yawning. "No" he said rubbing his eyes trying to stay awake. He sat there all night, waiting and listening, afraid and alone. He couldn't tell me how mum was feeling but I already knew, I felt it too.

119

He was worried, really worried. All night, he guarded her door, ensuring she wouldn't leave and possibly do something she'd later regret. Every shuffle or sigh from her room had him on edge, and he would peek in, just to be sure she was okay. The next morning, after Benjamin and I left for school, she finally stepped out of her room, finding Mweeka right there, waiting for her. His immediate response was, "Are you okay?" as he reached out to hold her hand.

"I'm fine son," she smiled, brushing past him to the bathroom. It was as if the previous night hadn't occurred. She didn't acknowledge his efforts, no hug, no thank you – nothing. Mweeka had spent a sleepless night, driven by the fear of "waking up without his mum," yet she seemed indifferent to it all.

I returned home to find her in high spirits, chatting on the phone and watching tennis. As I hesitantly greeted her with, "Hey mum…", she beckoned, "Hey daughter, sit with me," inviting me to join her.

"I know you're pretending to be okay," I said, turning towards her, searching for any hint of acknowledgment in her face. But she remained stoic, eyes fixed on the TV. Did she talk about her feelings to anyone, if not Mweeka or me? As I watched her, a realization struck – "I'm you," I whispered to myself. The emotions I buried deep, the nightmares, the anxiety, the sudden surges of anger – they all mirrored my mum. I was seeing in her what I felt inside me. She wanted to be strong for her babies, I get

120

it, the more I ages the more I realized that hiding your emotions isn't what makes you strong. You become stronger with transparency and expressing emotion to your loved ones.

After what seemed like endless arguments between my parents about who would keep us kids, dad came out on top. The decision was clear: I'd be with him while my brothers stayed with mum. Dad was doing well, much better than before. His temper had cooled, and our bond had strengthened. He'd even snagged a new house by the seaside. It was spacious, nestled next to streets lined with grand mansions that I loved gazing at during my walks. The house, a two-bedroom gem, was freshly built and untouched. It came with a garden, a driveway out front, an upstairs bathroom, a downstairs toilet, a storage room, and lovely interiors. The best part? I had my own room, a blank canvas that I was itching to personalize.

Living here felt right. For the first time, I was in a place where everything clicked. Yet, my thoughts often wandered to that boy I'd run into during summer. After some online detective work, I found him on Facebook. There he was, in a profile picture, surrounded by friends at a party, each holding a beer. He sported an awkward smile, like he was a bit shy of the camera, and his hair was perfectly styled. My heart raced as I hovered over the "add friend" button, thoughts whirling. "What if he sees it? Would he decline or accept?" With a surge of boldness, I clicked 'add friend' and immediately tossed my phone aside, reeling from my own audacity. I wasn't sure if he was attracted to girls like me, nor for my character or what I was interested in, or the music I listened to, I was fearful he didn't like girls with the same colour skin as me. The same facial features and Afro hair. The city I lived in was small, being black or pretty much any other race meant you were a minority, a lot of us were marginalized which was awful, so being seen and appreciated from a guy wasn't common to me.

The day Grandma Regina got sick was the darkest day I'd ever known. School wouldn't let me off early, so the minute the bell rang, I raced to the bus stop, heading straight for Lancaster Hospital where they'd taken her. Bursting into the reception, I pleaded, "I need to see her." She was only 50! How could life be so cruel to someone so full of it? But walking into her room, my heart sank. It was hard to recognize the vivacious woman I knew in the frail figure before me. Her arms, so thin, I could circle her wrist with just my thumb and index finger. She looked so fragile and weary. Slowly, I pulled up a chair next to her bed, taking her hand in mine, holding back the flood of tears threatening to spill.

That's when I learned the devastating news. She had cancer, and it was too advanced to treat. The weight of that revelation made subsequent hospital visits unbearable. So, whenever my mum went to see her, I'd make an excuse, too scared to face the inevitable goodbye. I couldn't muster the courage to accept that her time was limited, and it's a choice I've regretted ever since. But on the occasions, I did visit, our bond shone through. "We sat and talked for hours," reminiscing, laughing, and sometimes just sitting in companionable silence. I'd bring her favourite snacks, and we'd munch on them, cherishing the simple joy of being together. The last few

days were spent quiet, she could barely talk, move her hands, so I just sat there,

watching her sleep peacefully, holding her hands and praying for a miracle.

We had a few more days with her, and I planned for what I'd do for each day. I

wanted to make her last days special even though it broke me, I had to be strong for

her. Every moment she'd been there for me, now it was my turn to be strong for her.

After school, I hurried towards mum's house, looking forward to a heart-warming

evening at the hospital with Grandma Regina. Tossing off my shoes at the entrance

and leaving my bag behind, I immediately sensed something was off. The house was

unnervingly quiet—no familiar sound of the TV, mum's voice on the phone, or even

the sizzle of something cooking. "Hello?" My voice echoed hesitantly as I ventured

further inside.

As I climbed the stairs, my heart sank seeing my mum in tears, with Benjamin

lost in despair. Their grief hung thick in the air, rendering them silent and distant.

"What happened?" I asked, anxiety gripping me, but neither responded. They

seemed far away, trapped in their grief. The sight that met me in the next room

confirmed my worst fears. There she was, Grandma Regina, lifeless on the bed. My

heart broke as I murmured, "No...no..." We were supposed to have more time, more

moments. We had time, I had plans, there was so much in store for the next few days.

I didn't get a chance to say a proper goodbye, how will she know how much I loved

her if I didn't get to say goodbye. I collapsed on the floor like my world had been shattered. I couldn't handle it; it was too painful to look at her body. I failed to process her death for weeks, it was so surreal, I searched for ways to heal my heart, but nothing worked.

Everywhere felt chaotic. The world was a cacophony of noise and motion until I found solace by the beach. Wandering aimlessly, I finally stopped and perched on the rocks, letting the rhythmic sound of waves drown the world's clamour. Everything came to a halt. Overlooking the vast water, I whispered, "I'm so sorry, I failed you. You were my anchor, my guiding star. What is life without you?" Tears clouded my vision as I poured my heart out, feeling as if she were right beside me, listening. With the sun setting, the world around me darkened, but the thought of leaving that peaceful spot terrified me. What if I never felt this serene again? I let the lullaby of the waves lull me to sleep.

The jingle of my phone's alarm startled me awake. It read 7AM. "Oh no," I exclaimed, scrambling over the rocks and sprinting home. A dying phone showed missed calls from dad. I tiptoed into the house, avoiding creaky stairs, and slid under my covers. When dad asked about my whereabouts, I lied about staying with mum. It was easier that way. Sharing my grief with him felt like walking on eggshells; he never understood my pain, always reminding me to be "grateful for life" and to "just get over" hardships. Maybe he was right, maybe I needed to get over this but how do you get over grief, how do you get over the pounding thoughts in your mind of what ifs. How do you escape the looping memories of the person you just lost. How? ...

124

We had trial exams for school that I didn't study for, I just couldn't find the motivation to revise. The teacher asked the class if we were prepared but I sat there drowning in my chair knowing I didn't know what the test was about flipping through the trial exam, I drew a blank. A quick glance around, and it hit me - everyone else was already writing. Knowing I was beat, I resorted to my old friend: doodling. "Art was my expression," I always believed. Whenever the world got a bit much, I'd lose myself in a sketch or painting.

As we handed in our papers, lunch break began. Bethany peeked over at my phone and teased, "Who are you chatting with?" With a smirk, I replied, "You know that guy we spotted at the lakes last summer? The one with that bunch of friends?" I showed her his photo from Facebook. Beth was the kind of girl boys always noticed. Me? Not so much. But with this guy, it felt different. Our chats were refreshing; he saw the real me, even if we went to different schools and barely met in person.

As the bell rang, I took my time. I didn't share the next class with Beth, so I waited for the hallways to clear out. A few steps in, I noticed a group of girls, all huddled up, giggling and engrossed in their phones. I ignored them but they followed me down the hallway, my anxiety started to kick in, so I turned around and stopped "what are you laughing at" I said. "Is that a wig?" One of the girls said walking closer. "No leave me alone" I said turning my back to walk away. She grabbed my hair and pulled me to the ground and spat in my face "fix your hair your ugly nigger" she laughed. I stood up and pushed her, "ugly?" I said "ugly?" I pushed

her again. Her friends stopped laughing and looked scared, my body was shaking, I

was embarrassed and angry. The teacher walked onto the corridor in that moment

and witnessed me hit the girl, "right get to Mrs. Seddon's office" she yelled. The

group of girls ran to their class, and I stood there wiping the spit off my face. "No, I'm

not doing that" I replied to her stood there with her arms crossed looking down at me.

"What did you just say" she said. "I won't be doing that; they were being racist" I said

and walked away. "Get back here young lady!" The teacher shouted. I walked back

and our eyes were locked, she didn't intimidate me, she was a joke to me. "Fix your

attitude, and fix your uniform, you do not push people no matter what they have said.

Now get to the office". I told her about the racism I encountered, and she shrugged it

off like it was nothing. She let the girl get away happily with no repercussions, and

she disregarded how I felt.

CHAPTER FIFTEEN

The Illusion of Love

Exiting school, I bypassed the head office and hopped on the train. I didn't have enough money for a round trip to Manchester so I snook on the train and hid in the toilet till it was time to get off. There were a few hours of school left, it seemed like a good time to distract myself. So, there I was, in Pizza Hut, still in my school uniform, scrolling through Facebook videos. The waiter approached, pen poised, "What would you like to order?" I looked up, flashing a grin, "Just charging my phone." She gave me a brief, assessing look and moved on.

Although school tried ringing mum, predictably she didn't pick up. They never thought to call dad - they weren't updated on me living with him. In a way, it was a relief. Mum, always preoccupied, rarely tuned into my school life. Dad? He'd have made it an issue. I wanted to navigate this on my own terms.

Once my phone was charged, I left Pizza Hut and quickly realized I was out of my depth. Manchester was sprawling compared to Lancaster. Trying to recall my steps, I wandered aimlessly, looking for the train station. Pulling out my phone for some Google Maps guidance, a young guy bumped into me. My phone clattered to the ground. "Oh, sorry!" He scooped it up, handing it back. "What's your name?" he asked. "Donny," I replied, still a bit flustered. He kindly offered to guide me back to the station. As we approached, he popped the unexpected question, "Can I get your number?" It caught me off guard, but I shrugged, thinking, "Why not?" and shared it. I gave him my number and forgot he existed, when I got home in time before my dad was back from work, I received a message from him. It wrote "hey beautiful" I stared at it for a while and wondered how I would reply to such a message. I ended up ignoring it and continued to scroll on my phone.

Days ticked by and Ross hadn't messaged me, though I saw him posting pictures on Facebook. Feeling a sting of rejection, I opened up to my friends. "He's got a girlfriend now," one of them blurted out. I blinked, taken aback, "He does?" She nodded, surprise evident on her face, "Haven't you heard?" I was shaken to the core, especially when I saw who the girl was. My heart dropped. She was the kind everyone admired, always looking flawless, dressed to the nines. Plus, she was white.

Growing up, my parents didn't dish out compliments about my looks. They showed love in other ways - paying rent, ensuring we had clothes, and reminding us that despite our financial struggles, our life in the UK was still leagues better than back in Africa. I wasn't ungrateful; I knew the lengths they'd gone to, the sacrifices made, just to feed us. "How could I complain?" I often thought. I firmly believe that the presence and influence of a father figure shapes a woman profoundly, especially when it comes to relationships. I didn't receive soft love from my dad, he didn't compliment my clothing choices, or clap for my appearance, or uplift my self-esteem.

Instead, he grabbed it all, threw it on the ground, stamped on it then wondered how his baby girl could turn out to be so insecure.

My dad, he always had something to say about my weight. "You're getting fat," he'd comment, even though I was just a young girl, my body changing and growing. "Look at the others your age, they're slim. You're just eating too much," he'd chide. Whether we were driving to school or sitting at the dinner table, he'd lecture me about weight. He'd caution me to eat slower, label me greedy, and sometimes, he'd even hide food from me in the house. Despite his comfortable job, structured savings, and a home that was objectively nicer than my mum's, I despised being there. Sure, he was organized and did things around the house, like cooking and gardening, to make it feel like a home, but it never really felt like mine.

At mum's house, things were different but was similar at the same time. I didn't feel a warmth and comfort since she was always working, and my brothers were doing their own thing. The truth is, I didn't feel like I belonged anywhere. My dad? He was often brooding, lost in his work, or heading out with his friends. We hardly spent any quality time, and most days, I'd stay locked up in my room. "A home isn't just about the building, it's about the energy and love that comes from it," I'd often think, feeling so alone and out of place there. It didn't feel like love with him; it felt like an obligation.

One evening, I was chatting with Beth on FaceTime, diving into the latest school gossip. It was our little escape, especially since we weren't usually part of the drama. Once our call ended, I felt this urge to change something about myself, to feel prettier. But how? I couldn't afford new clothes or makeup, and honestly, I didn't even know the first thing about applying it! So, I asked my friend Shelby if she wanted to meet in town the next day after school. Shelby was a girl in our friendship group who was outgoing, outspoken, and didn't follow rules. She was fun to be around but was very mischievous. I wanted to look in the mirror and liked what I seen, I wanted to change myself desperately, I thought if I looked better, if I looked like they do, they would see me.

School had just wrapped up, and I found myself waiting for Shelby by the entrance. Shelby and I, we didn't share any classes since she was placed in the lower group due to her behaviour. I never wanted to be in that group; it was mostly kids who didn't seem to care about what came next in life. Beth stood beside me, chatting away. Soon, Shelby burst through the doors, and the three of us made our way to the town centre.

As we wandered around the beauty shop, I leaned over to Shelby, "I'm going to snag a lipstick, keep an eye out," I whispered. I nonchalantly strolled down the aisle, glancing at the array of lipsticks. Carefully, I edged closer, swiftly pocketed a bold red lipstick, and re-joined the girls. Grinning, I whispered to Shelby, "Smooth, right?" She chuckled and followed suit. That day, our little shopping "spree" didn't stop at just lipstick. There were eye shadows, foundations, eyeliners, and blushes.

The bus ride home? It was buzzing with excitement. "I couldn't wait to get home, put on the makeup, snap a new profile picture, and show it off online." I hustled back home, eager to dive into my new makeup collection. I plopped down by my mirror, pulled up YouTube on my phone, and played a tutorial titled, "How to do your makeup." Let's be real, it wasn't easy. I kept pausing, rewinding, and trying again. An hour later, I looked different. A good kind of different. Stunning, even.

Taking a moment, I thought, "Why not capture this?" So, I perched on my bed, phone in hand. But looking down, I felt that my hoodie didn't match the glam vibe. Quickly changing into a pink T-shirt from my drawer, I snapped that perfect selfie and uploaded it.

The anxious wait began. The first notification pinged, and it was a like. Then another, and another. "People were liking the photo!" That validation, it's like a shot of confidence. For the first time, I felt, well, truly beautiful. I've always been self-conscious about my smile, thanks to that gap between my teeth. It seemed unique, not something I'd seen on others. So, I rarely smiled in photos. The fact that my pic got 40 likes? It felt like a major win. Beth usually got 100 or more likes on hers, with loads of comments. Seeing none on mine stung a bit, but hey, Snapchat was the "in thing" back then, and it felt great to be a part of that wave. I didn't post my face on my story only funny videos with my friends. I took a selfie for my Snap chat story for the first time but received no messages, I deleted it because people viewed it but didn't care enough to reply. I was lying in bed insecure, unsure, and doubting my beauty, so I replied to the text message I received from the guy I bumped into in Manchester. "Hello" I texted him. He replied rarely quick, so I sat up in bed thinking of what to say. "Do you think I'm pretty?" I asked him. He was typing for a while, so I thought he was struggling to think of words to say. He texted back with a paragraph of compliments, telling me how 'gorgeous' I am, and that date made us bump into each other, he told me I was the best-looking girl he had ever seen. I sat on the edge of my bed reading the wonderful things he was saying, I couldn't believe it, someone thinks I'm pretty.

No one had ever noticed me before, or better yet expressed their love for me in the way he did. That evening when we texted it felt like my heart was glowing, he said everything I never heard from anyone before. It was 3 hours later, and we were still texting, his replies were quick, 'I have all his attention' I thought to myself. He asked to speak on the phone, but I was nervous, so we continued our conversation on text instead. I asked how old he was, and he took a while to reply, it had gone 20 minutes and he didn't reply to my message. I was confused, his replies were so fast before why they would stop now. "I'm 23 is that okay sweetheart I love you so much" he texted back. I knew he was slightly older than me from our first encounter, but I had no idea he was that much older. I texted him and told him I'm 13 years old. It didn't faze him, in fact he encouraged it.

So, he had this theory that girls mature faster when they're young, and they need older guys to guide them, you know? Saying that young boys are still figuring things out and don't bring much to the table. We chatted for days, and one morning, I even found myself chatting with him on the phone on my way to school. He insisted on keeping our talks a secret, and I went along with it. It was like I had this private little world nobody could touch – not my family, not my friends, no one. He talked a lot about his fancy job at a sports betting company, bragging about the big bucks he made and the shiny car he drove. He even dangled the idea of whisking me away for a posh meal in Manchester sometime.

Then, one afternoon, he texted me an address, somewhere I'd never been. Turns out, it was this car park near the town centre. There, in the middle of it all, was this sleek black car, and guess who was in the driver's seat? It was him. As I got closer, he waved, and when I hopped in, we shared a hug. From the back, he pulled out this fancy-looking gift bag. Inside was a shiny silver necklace. I remember saying, "Wow, thank you. This must've cost a lot." And he was like, "I'll always look out for you. Forget pinching makeup, I can get it for you." His gesture, it felt genuine and sweet. We sat there, chatting away, until I realized it was getting late. He suggested a drive, but I knew I had to beat dad home. I dashed to the bus stop, made it just in time, and headed back. The following day, Beth invited me over, and I loved hanging

133

out at her place. It always felt so welcoming. She put music on, and we sat and talked. I wanted to tell her about the new guy I met, that I no longer cared about the crushes I had.

I wanted to spill the beans to Beth, really, I did. But I kept thinking, how do I even start? How do I tell her that the boys I crush on only seem to notice girls who look like her – blonde, dressed in fancy stuff? I felt like if I told her they don't see girls like me, she just wouldn't get it. Riley was Nigerian, and to be honest, I didn't know much about him – where he lived, if he had any siblings. He was all hush-hush about himself, while I was an open book. But the mystery was kind of thrilling. So, I chose to keep it to myself, our little secret.

School was a blur of sneaky texts. Most times, during class, my phone would be sneakily resting on my lap, buzzing with Riley's latest message. Once during lunch, Shelby caught me grinning at a text and probed, "Who's got you smiling like that?" Panicking, I quickly locked my phone, "Oh, just watching a funny video," I bluffed.

Riley had this plan for after school, told me to pack an outfit so I could ditch my school uniform. When the final bell rang, I darted to the loo to change. Soon after, I found myself at that same familiar car park, spotting his car. We'd had a pretty deep chat recently – I'd told him about how I wasn't ready for anything physical. Call it a cultural thing, or just personal, but I wanted to save certain intimacies for my husband. And he seemed to get it. He made me feel alright about it, saying we could just get to know each other, no rush.

With Riley, I felt valued. He listened when I was down, was there when I needed a pick-me-up, and never failed to remind me how beautiful I was. This was a stark contrast to home where Mum wasn't the affectionate type and Dad? He'd take any chance to put me down. With Riley, I felt seen. And the future? According to him, it looked like pure gold.

That day, we drove for what felt like ages and landed at a restaurant. Oddly, he'd mentioned it was close by. Before heading in, he dropped this line, "If anyone asks, say you're my sister." Puzzled, I questioned it, but he just brushed it off saying it was part of our secret. Inside, I tried reaching out for his hand, but he dodged and led the way. At our table, I noticed the waitress giving me these weird looks. Couldn't fathom why, but it had me feeling out of place. As we chatted and ate, I felt the need to touch up my lipstick, so I excused myself to the restroom. Inside the restroom, the waitress followed, casually pretending to wash her hands. "Are you okay?" she asked, locking eyes with mine through the mirror's reflection. I replied, "Yes, I'm okay, thank you," while reapplying my lipstick. But she wasn't buying it. Turning towards me, she said firmly, "Look, if you need some help, let me know." She scribbled her number on my palm using the pen from her apron. I didn't know how to react, so I just offered a smile and walked out to Riley who whispered, "You look beautiful."

Once outside, the sun was painting the sky with shades of twilight. "Give me your phone," Riley suddenly demanded. Puzzled, I asked, "Why?" His reasoning was that he didn't want me to get tempted to capture any moments of us. I assured him that wasn't my intention, but he wouldn't budge. So, I handed it over, wanting him to see he could trust me. The thing is people warn you about dangerous situations. They guide you on what red flags to watch out for. But nobody ever really prepares you for those times when love clouds judgement, where your heart drowns out reason. There's no guidebook on handling love so intense that it blinds you to the glaring signs.

The car roared to life, but there was an unusual silence. No music. I tried making conversation, but Riley's responses were terse. I brushed it off, thinking he might be upset over the phone ordeal, and turned to look outside. The landscape seemed unfamiliar. Noticing this, I remarked, "This doesn't look like the way back. Are you sure you're going the right way?" Without missing a beat, he replied, "I took a shorter way to get you back home quicker."

CHAPTER SIXTEEN

The Silence of Shadows

After a few more minutes driving he stopped the car and parked up by a big park. "You upset me; you didn't give me the phone like I asked the first time" he said. "I'm sorry, it won't happen again" I said. He got out the car "where are you going?" I said to him while getting out the car. I grabbed my bag and put it on the roof of the car, I stood there asking him to stop walking away "You don't love me, do you?" He stopped walking and turned to me. "Of course, I do" I said. "You have to show me you love me" he said. I stood there confused for a moment silent. He huffed and continued walking. He walked and walked and walked, all the way down deep into the park ignoring me. "Stop talking we can talk" I said. "Can you at least take me home I don't know where I am" I said "Riley can I have my phone I'm getting scared" I said. My countless efforts didn't work, and I started to feel worried the deeper into the park we got. "STOP" I shouted.

He immediately stopped walking and paced towards me. He reached his hands out and squeezed my face "shut the fuck up, someone will hear you" he said. My face was hurting, his hands were strong, I tried taking his hands off my face, but it didn't budge. He let go and stared at me blankly "show me you love me" he said. "I can't I don't know what you mean" I replied to him. He was losing his temper, he looked around, put his hands on his head and was breathing heavy. "Can I just go home" I said. "Home? Home? I just spent money on you. I just took you to a restaurant for a meal and you can't even show me you love me" he said angrily close to my face. He grabbed my arm and threw me to the ground. My clothes were getting muddy as I tried to stand up. He stood over me and pulled his trousers down, then put his foot on my leg as I tried to stand.

He lowered his body over me and grabbed my T-shirt, "if you scream, I'll kill you" he said. My body went into shock, and I didn't know what to do, I looked around to try see if by one was near but there was nobody in sight. It was dark and I had no idea where I was at. I attempted to push his body off, but he was too heavy, he put his knees on my legs and pulled my leggings down. I closed my eyes and prayed to God; he would help me. He put his hand over my mouth when I started to scream then hit me multiple times in the face demanding I be quiet. He kept his hand on my mouth, and reached down with his other hand, I could feel his hands on my body, and I started to cry. I turned my head, but it was difficult with his hands on my face, I got a glance of a rock to my left, so I pulled and released my hand, grabbed the rock and hit him with it across the face.

My legs were then slightly released giving me enough room to wiggle out of the position I was in. I kicked my legs repeatedly until I was no longer pulled down. He held his head in agony and quickly got up and ran. I blanked out at this moment, I was so fearful and afraid, but all I could do was run. I ran so fast like I had never run before. I reached the entrance to the park and caught sight of his car. I pulled the door handle, but it wasn't opening, I looked inside the car but couldn't see my phone. 'He must have it in his pocket' I thought to myself. As I grabbed my bag from the roof of the car I glanced inside and noticed his work badge in the back seat, I was lost for words. His name badge didn't say Riley.... It said "Obaloluwa" I will never forget that name I saw that day. I could see him slowly walking closer from the distance, still holding his head, so I knew my time to run was short.

I ran down the road, down a street and lost him. I looked at my hand and noticed the number that was written on my palm. 'I need to get to a phone' I thought to myself. I went to the nearest house and knocked on the door "help me" I said. There was no answer. I tried the next house "someone help me", there was no answer. I was losing breath and I was getting more tired as the minutes went by. I knocked on the next-door panting "help me" the door opened, and a woman was stood there looking at me up and down. "What do you want I don't have money" she said. I was panting and struggling for air "no. ma'am. I need to use your phone I'm in danger" I said trying to get my words out. "Is this the new trick you blacks are coming up with? Go and rob someone else's house!"

She said while slamming the door in my face. I walked down the street and began feeling dizzy, my body was exhausted, and I desperately needed water. I fell to the ground and thankfully a woman walking her dog immediately stopped to help. "Oh my gosh sweetheart is you okay" she said kneeling down. She helped me up and allowed me to use her phone. I dialed the number that was on my hand and the waitress picked up. "Hello, how may I help". I explained to her what happened. I caught her just in time when she was heading home from work. The lady with the dog stayed with me until she came to my rescue.

139

I was in so much shock I could barely think straight, I was stuttering my words and it was cold. The waiter pulled up in her car and drove me to the nearby train station, gave me some cash for the ticket home. I didn't tell her the full story I was ashamed because I knew it was my fault, why would I be so naive, how didn't I spot the red flags, what's wrong with me. I got on the train and sat down, when I looked out the window, she was still stood there making sure I was safely boarding. There were people on the train looking at me strangely, I looked down and realized I was covered in mud, my leggings had holes in them, and my T-shirt was slightly torn. I rushed to the toilet on the train with my school bag and took out my uniform. I brushed my hair and used the sink to wash my face.

I took off my clothes and looked in the mirror, I was covered in bruises and marks. I stood there lifting my arms up, turning my back and analyzing my body. I quickly put my uniform on, washed my hands, scrunched up my leggings and T-shirt then walked out of the toilet. I looked around and everyone was minding their business on the train, it was quite empty, so I slowly sat on an empty seat, stuffed my clothes under the seat, then sat in a different carriage. I stared outside the window and cried silently. The tears didn't stop, it was like a someone stabbed me in my heart with a sword. I wanted to erase the memory in my head, I felt disgusting, dirty, and gross. Every time I shut my eyes I could feel his breath on my face, his hand covering mouth, the weight of his body onto of me and the excruciating pain from the pressure of him attempting to force his penis inside of me.

The thought was so severe I wanted to nothing but get home and scrub myself clean, go to sleep and pretend that it didn't happen. It was getting late, and I was worried if my dad had tried to call me since I don't have my phone. When I arrived home the door was locked, and I didn't have my key. I rang the doorbell and waited patiently. He came to the door and looked furious. "It's 10pm" he said with his arms crossed. I had never seen such anger in his eyes before. "I'm so sorry dad I will explain". He was silent, he walked inside the house and I followed him inside. I was so nervous to tell him, I didn't know where to start. I played different conversation starters in my head a few times as we were walking inside.

I headed straight to my room and began taking my uniform off preparing for a shower. I took my blazer off when I could hear rusting coming from the front room. My dad was searching for something, but I didn't know what, as I was about to take my school skirt off, he stormed into my room. He had a long thick wire in his hand and his feet stomped the floor. He grabbed my wrists and pulled my body down to the bed. I flinched in pain because my body was still sore. "You want to stay out late with your friends" he said pinning me down to the bed. My dad is a 6'3 male, slim build and he was very strong, no matter how much I tried to move nothing worked, I was skinny and frail, my body experienced trauma and I was fatigued, I had no energy. "I wasn't with my friends I promise you I can explain" I cried out for him to stop.

He called me a liar and lashing me with the cable cord. I put my arms to my face to protect myself, he whipped me for the second time, the more he did it the harsher it got. "Please dad stop" I yelled. His anger was fueled by the disappointment of his son, he thought I was like him, I wasn't. He was furious and had

no remorse. His heart was empty, he didn't have any love for me. He repeated lashed

me with the tough cable with his entire strength, when I tried to get up, he pushed me

down to the bed and continued. I yelled at the top of my voice hoping the neighbours

could hear me. He expressed his hatred for me as he put his entire force in the

whips. The cable had a tough metal end, which caught me a few times. I was slowly

losing consciousness, I put my arms down because my muscles were sore, but he

continued, I couldn't fight back any longer, but he continued. I laid there silently

crying, till he stopped. It lasted so long my entire body was shaking, I looked at the

floor searching for my bag, I could see he dropped the cable, so I knew he was

finished.

I pushed my body off the bed and crawled to my bag, I used the wall for

support to stand up, put my art book in my bag and stood by the door silently. I put

my head around the corner, his bedroom door was shut, and it was my chance to

run. I grabbed my shoes and walked out the house as quickly as I could, dragging

my feet on the floor and trying to keep my balance. I opened the door slowly and

quietly, then left a crack in the door so it didn't make a sound when I closed it. I got to

the bus stop and knelt to put my shoes on. My ribs were aching, everything was

hurting. Thankfully the bus came as soon as my shoes were on, and I paid to head to

my mum's house. The bus ride was so fast, I couldn't recollect my thoughts. When I

arrived at my mum's house, I went straight to her room and laid on the bed, I curled my legs up to my chest and cried. "What's wrong" my mum said walking into the room and sitting on the bed.

I looked at her face with tears falling down my face and couldn't tell her that her baby girl had endured so much that day. I told her I had an argument with my dad, and she told me to rest. She headed off to work and I stayed in her bed alone, with nothing but a wet pillow full of my tears. I wanted to avoid school the following day, I couldn't handle going into that building full of kids shouting and teachers being miserable. My mum came home from work in the morning and told me it wasn't an option to stay home so I waited till she exited the room so I could get out of bed. I didn't want her to see the damage that was done to my body. I tried to stand up, but it was too hard, I counted to three and got up on my feet, walked to the mirror and lifted my T-shirt. I was covered in wounds, the whip marks were so severe they thickened and swelled up, I had scratches on my neck and arms that had dried blood around them from the metal part of the cable lashing me so hard it pierced my skin. My thighs were covered in harsh bruises from being sexually assaulted, and my arms and legs had immense muscle pain from fighting back.

It was PE that day, and I knew I would have to wear shorts and short sleeve which would reveal to everyone my marks. Going to school that day felt dark, it was a numb feeling, I didn't know how I got there, I was just there, I didn't know what my friends spoke about, or what colour the sky was, or how I got dressed. I wasn't present in the moment; I was just getting by. I was in the changing room trying to think of ways I could avoid PE. I went into the PE office and told the teacher my

143

period was too heavy so I couldn't preform, they said it wasn't a good enough excuse so told me I had to do it anyway. I ran to the toilets with my bag and stayed there, I refused to take my clothes off, I could imagine people's faces if they saw me. The most brutal thing about being abused by someone you love is it makes you feel unworthy.

For so long, I grappled with the idea of love. I thought, "If the person who created me couldn't love me, then why would a stranger?" Such feelings and thoughts often leave a void, and people try to fill it in different ways. Some turn to addiction, and some seek love – but not the gentle, comforting kind. It's the love that's loud and chaotic, stemming from insecurities and memories of a 'deadbeat' dad. It's the sort of love that draws you in only to push you away. I vowed to myself never to speak of that day. The experience haunted me – worsening my nightmares and making me startle at the slightest touch.

A month passed, and I hadn't heard from my dad. I was staying with my mum, which was actually alright. When Mweeka visited, I confided in him about that dreadful day with dad. I shared my pain, both emotional and physical. To my dismay, he thought I deserved it, claiming I should've been home earlier and that it was discipline. He believed a parent's physical punishment was discipline, but to me, it felt like torture. We look to our parents for guidance, hoping they'll set an example. So, what if that guidance is riddled with adversity, toxicity, and abuse? Disappointed with Mweeka's reaction, I held onto my decision to keep silent. I'd thought he'd be the one person who'd understand, and since he didn't, I was sure I'd never speak of it again.

One day, from my bedroom window, I saw my dad parked outside mum's house. As I watched, he hesitated for a while before finally knocking. Mum called me down, saying he wanted to see me. He greeted me with a smile, suggesting a trip to the town centre for new trainers. I couldn't fathom how he could act so casual after everything. But, deep down, part of me still longed for my dad. He got me those shoes I'd been eyeing for weeks. It wasn't a verbal apology, but his gesture spoke volumes. I wasn't ready to move back with him, so I thanked him for the shoes and returned to mum's place. He dropped off most my clothes and I said his goodbyes. It was quite nice staying at my mum's house, I got to be free to do what I liked, and the best way to get over my hardship was to get drunk.

CHAPTER SEVENTEEN

Struggles at Home and Unlikely Friendships

It was the talk of the town: a huge party at the local park, and every school was going to be there that weekend. I just had to join in. Beth and I managed to sneak out, got dressed up, and hit the town. We found ourselves outside a shop, hoping to rope in some adult to buy us vodka. "After the 2 hours mission of waiting around," we finally got our bottle and made our way to the park. It was packed, with a mix of familiar and new faces. We found our crowd and settled in, soaking up the vibes, everyone was drunk or on drugs. The night was a blend of laughter, wild games, and booming music. I couldn't help but notice some of the popular girls sneaking kisses with boys in a corner. There were phones out, recording and cheering. I thought, "This is going to be all everyone talks about at school."

As the night progressed, the alcohol took a toll on me, and I ended up throwing up behind a bush. That's when Benjamin spotted me. "What are you doing here?" he questioned, scanning the surroundings. He insisted, "Go home now." Benjamin was always like that - protective, just like any big brother. His presence was comforting, even if it meant dealing with his 'big brother' lectures. During the park party, I was using an old phone my friend had given me, a kind gesture, especially since I hadn't told her the whole story about what happened to my previous one. When I walked home drunk, I was typing on the phone but clueless who I was having a conversation with to realize it was Ross. He replied to my story of me drunk and

said I should get home safe. I stopped walking and looked at the phone closely and

smiled.

It was pitch dark, and I stood frozen on the street, my phone's glow

illuminating my face. "Looking at his message," my heart raced. Continuing my walk

home, I was caught off guard by an unfamiliar face in our kitchen. "Who are you?" I

blurted out at the sight of the unknown man. He lifted a beer can, replying, "I'm your

mum's friend, Lee."

Apparently, Mum rented out our third bedroom to him to help with finances.

This meant I now had to bunk with Benjamin. Not ideal, especially since we were at

that age where we craved our own space. Lee was, well, scruffy, to put it mildly.

Every word he spoke carried the stench of stale beer, making me hold my breath.

Mum's reasoning for having Lee was clear: bills were piling up. I was envious of other

kids who received new things daily, they were well-off who wore designer clothes and

celebrated their Christmas and birthdays in style. While we made do, they lived it up.

It didn't seem fair to me, having to live in the council estate house, wearing the same

clothes on rotate and having to make every penny count.

Mum always painted a rosy picture of our life in the UK, especially when

speaking to relatives in Africa. I didn't push her about having a lodger, simply grateful

for the roof above. Beth would sometimes visit, and despite my apprehensions about our home's state compared to hers, she was non-judgmental. She even embraced our African meals. The room Benjamin and I shared was a work in progress, with half-painted walls and a still wet paintbrush in one corner. Remnants of our younger days, like a bunk bed scribbled with drawings and a half-torn poster, filled the space.

Kicking back on our well-used swivel chair, I spun around while Beth lounged on the bed. "So, what do you want to do today?" I asked, still spinning. "Why don't we go to McDonald's?" she suggested. The local McDonald's was a go-to hangout spot. It wasn't about the food, but just a place to chill and be on our phones. Chatting with Ross on Snapchat during our walk there, he dispelled rumours of him having a girlfriend. A wave of relief hit me. Maybe, just maybe, it was my shot with him. All the girls in my year group were hooking up, or having boyfriends, but it was against my culture to behave in that manner, so I wanted to wait for the perfect person, he was my perfect person. I wasn't brave enough to open up about my feelings for him, so I joked him instead. I was still so fearful of men, what if he's going to hurt me? Every time I would give myself a pep talk to tell him how I feel, those flashbacks would come back and taunt me, sabotaging the chance I had to be with the boy of my dreams. Trauma ruins your perspective on life, it ruins your chances, it strips you away from what could be. It isn't about the event, it's about the after. It's about the walls that are built too stubborn to tear down. Trauma waits patiently in the shadows, waiting for the perfect moment to ruin a 'good thing'. He was my good thing. We were sat in McDonald's when I noticed eyes were on me, there was a group of girls from

Ripley high school staring at me and screwing their face. The school was full of snobby girls with daddy's money. I could overhear them mocking me for what I wore. "What is she even wearing" they laughed to each other. It didn't offend me so much as words like that used to. I stared back at them and told them if they kept on staring, I'd rip their eyes out and ruin their vision. They immediately stopped laughing and turned away. I smiled feeling proud, I felt touch and invincible. I went home that evening to find Lee drinking beer in the kitchen, I glanced at him then continued walking to the front room.

I was tired and fell asleep on the couch with the TV on. My mum went to work, and Benjamin was out with his friends as usual. I was fast asleep, deep in my dreams at peace. I woke up to the feel of someone's hand under my clothes. I could smell Lee's hot beer breathe in my face and I froze as I opened my eyes. My flashbacks started and I was nervous, my body was heating up and I could feel sweat dripping down my face. "What. what are you doing?" I spoke. "Shhh! It's okay" he said slurring his words. He had taken my top off in my deep sleep, leaving the top half of my body completely nude. His hands were in my shorts, touching me. I couldn't move a muscle; the fear was flowing through my body as if it completely shut down. I closed my eyes and pictured the ice cream van, the order and sitting down on the bench looking at the flower field. It was working, it helped me calm my heart rate down. I jumped up and pushed him off me. I was vulnerable, weak. I had no power in me, and I hated myself for it.

He stood up and pulled his pants up, "what did you do to me" I said with my voice breaking. He walked to the kitchen swaying as he walked ignoring me. I followed him into the kitchen and hit the can of beer that was in his hand, and it split everywhere. "I made myself cum over the feel of your pretty little black body are you happy" he said opening another can of beer.

"You did what" I said pushing him. "Go on hit me then what are you going to do with your little self, aye" he replied. I dressed myself, stormed out of the house, and walked down the street with my hand on my chest. My heart was beating tremendously, it felt like I was having a heart attack, I was overwhelmed, upset, violated, confused, sad. The gushing waves of emotions were taking over, and I could no longer gather my thoughts properly. The place I was supposed to feel protected and safe was the place I feared to stay. There was a bridge in front of me, it was the answer to my problems, it was just what I needed. I walked up the stairs panting for air, taking one step at a time till I finally got to the top. I looked over the railing at the dark water. I couldn't see a thing. My vision was blurred by my tears. I questioned if God was really with me, if he even cared to keep me safe. Where was he when I needed him. Where was he now? I stood on that bridge looking down with a million questions running through my mind.

They say that people who commit suicide are selfish, how could you do such a thing to your family? How could you leave behind the ones that love you? I was hurting inside, and the thought of living for longer was too painful to bare, with so much sadness how could I possibly think about someone else, I just wanted to leave.

I just wanted to be free from my pain. I looked over that bridge at the city lights, "I want to burn it all" I said. I didn't know how I was going to overcome the obstacles that were so severe, but that night I had to just try. I didn't choose to carry on living because the thought of death was unknown and scary, I chose to carry on living because of the possibility of life getting better. You see the thing is when you experience battles, everything collapses.

Your whole word comes crashing down, then you see your friend with a smile on their face waiting for you to get on the bus and that feeling goes away for a split moment. You want to scream and shout, then you feel the warm embrace of someone you love dearly. I chose to chase those thrills in life than give in the horrors and tormenting shadows of my experiences, because those thrills were all the reason to keep living. I knew my mum needed the money, so I stayed silent about the situation, I wanted to put her needs before mine. She didn't deserve to go through the trouble of finding someone else to rent the room... at least that's what I told myself.

Turning 15 felt like a new chapter. With each passing year, school seemed harder, but I was determined that this year would be different - filled with new experiences and me taking some risks. Ross and I became inseparable, hanging out in Morecambe and dreaming about the future. Sometimes I'd catch myself thinking, "What if I told him how his blue eyes make my heart skip a beat?" Ross was the life of the party. He had this way of making everyone laugh, singing in funny voices and acting wild.

As the end of school approached, I noticed my grades slipping. Art was the only subject I seemed to excel in. I didn't let it bother me too much because I knew I wanted to chase a creative path. But every Parents' Day, I'd see the disappointment in my mum's eyes as teachers would tell her about my struggles. She hoped I'd become a doctor or a nurse, dreaming bigger for me than she had for herself. It's a thing with a lot of parents; sometimes they see their kids as a second shot at their own dreams. For me, I wasn't quite sure about my future, but I knew one thing for sure: I wanted to succeed.

Teachers drilled into us that success meant good grades. Growing up in an environment where wealth seemed out of reach, I started believing them.

Then, there was the day I went to school with my natural hair. Mum always made sure my hair was braided or under a wig, saying it was to look "presentable", but deep down, I felt she was shielding me from being teased. But that day, she didn't have time. Walking into science class late, I felt every eye on me. Josie's laughter echoed, mocking my Afro. The rest of the class wasn't any kinder, flicking pens to see if they'd stick in my curls. It was a long day. When it was lunchtime people gathered around me and asked to touch my hair, it made me feel different from them. I felt like I was some strange animal that entered the school, everyone had their eyes on me and pulled weird faces, they touched my hair and said it felt weird or made comments referring it to sheep hair or a microphone. Someone took a photo of me and uploaded it online to mock me further. I seen it when I got home, and I was devastated. I couldn't help my hair length or texture, so why should I be tormented for it? My brother caught wind of what was happening and didn't let it past him. Benjamin was the type of brother that had my back, always. He got onto his bike and rode to the town centre where the boy would hang around.

He confronted him, told him to delete the picture but he refused so my brother threatened to beat him up. He started running away from Benjamin, but Benjamin caught him quickly with his fast pace and beat him up, made him delete the photo and forced him to apologize to me on social media. The boy had a black eye and even though I didn't want violence to occur, he deserved it. After this day the racism slowed down majorly, people knew my brother didn't care who you were, how old you were, your gender, your background, if you were mean to me, it was a disrespect to him.

I was looking forward to a house party that a popular girl was hosting at her house because her parents wasn't home, I couldn't wait to have fun with Beth and make some friends. Everyone at school was talking about the huge party going on at the weekend and what they were going to wear. They were talking about going into town and buying a new outfit for the party, but I knew I wouldn't have enough money to get something to wear. When school ended, I walked to the town centre and into a store that sold pretty outfits, there was a nice dress that would look pretty on me, but it was £60. If I asked my mum for it, she would have had the same reply "money is tight right now", I asked to to a pile of clothes on and the dress at the bottom, when I

153

got into the changing room, I stuffed the dress in my bag and walked out. "I don't want them they don't fit" I said, while handing over the pile of clothes to the lady working at the dressing room desk.

When I got home, I put the dress on and took the tag off, it was gorgeous. It hugged me tight and was paired with a pair of heels I begged my mum for which only costs £5 from Primark. When I arrived at the party on the weekend with Beth the music was good, I walked in and was greeted with open arms. It was almost as if… people accepted me, not only that but they saw me! We did our vodka in the room upstairs so nobody could find it and drink any. I was enjoying the night with Beth, dancing to the music but needed the bathroom so I headed upstairs. I walked into the wrong room and there were people sniffling lines of cocaine, I walked into another room and people were passed out on the floor and on the bed.

I finally found the toilet, I was drunk and sat there with my head swaying side to side. The feeling of being intoxicated was calming. I couldn't feel anything other than the bass of the music downstairs and the blood pumping through my body. Everything was slow yet fast all at once and in that moment, I felt good. I wasn't worried about school, exams or my grades, my parents arguing over the phone, or my mum stressing about the bills or traumatic experiences, I was just young, drunk, in a girls house I never spoke to before throwing up in her toilet then walking down her steps barefoot after taking my heels off and dancing on her couch. It was a moment to be alive, an escape from reality just for a night, then I'd wake up with a blasting headache, the curtains close and my eyes burning from the brightness of my phone, scrolling through social media replaying back the fun memories of a good night.

I was happy to spend my evening at home watching films when I received a message on Facebook from one of the popular girls who invited me to a party. It was a weekend, and my mum wasn't home, so it was a perfect opportunity to go and have fun. I wore jeans and a cute top, did my hair and set off. Listening to music while heading out was my favourite thing to do, it pumped me up and got me ready. I didn't have enough money for a taxi, so I got on the bus to the location instead. My music was on full blast, walking down the street excited to have a good night. I could hear low pitched voices, so I removed my earphones and turned around to see a group of boys walking my direction. I paced myself and walked quicker but every time I looked back; I wasn't too far from them. I turned my music off, put my earphones in my pocket and pretended to be on the phone. I could feel them getting closer, so I began panicking.

They were shouting football chants, throwing beer cans on the street and yelling "we don't like niggers" then laughing. A boy in a red jacket and Adidas trainers ran in front of me and stopped. I attempted to walk past him, but he put his arms out to stop me. His friendship group crowded around me continuing to chant football songs and waving an England flag. I looked at the ground and told him to move out my way, "you're a little nigger aren't you" he said laughing then looking at his friends for approval. Most of them laughed apart from a few who looked at each other and lifted their eyebrows in shock. "Leave her alone Tommy" one of them said.

155

"Yeah, fuck off" I said trying to walk past him. I was rarely intimidated by strangers on the street, but this time I was outnumbered, especially because they were all boys.

I could fight girls and defend myself, but with boys or men they put fear in me, it was like I was inferior to them, so I knew I had no chance. "Who the fuck are you talking to" he said while pushing me. I looked around but they all watched without making efforts to stop him. "You going to hit a girl?" I said stepping back from him. "I wouldn't consider a monkey a girl" he said, they all started laughing, I felt humiliated.

I tried to walk away from them, but they circled me and pushed me to towards him every time I tried. He lifted his arm into the air above my head and said "watch this lads" looking at his friends. I looked up and in a split second he poured beer all over me. It went in my hair and soaked all my clothes. When I tried to move away his friend pushed me back till the entire beer can was empty. He threw the can at me, and his friends moved away, so I ran back home in tears. I heard someone shout "wait". Turning back, I seen one of the boys who was present run up to me "here have this" he said passing me his football scarf, "wipe yourself down. I'm sorry about my mate he's off his head, he does this shit all the time and I always tell him it ain't right. He doesn't listen, I promise I'm not a racist cunt like him get home safe yeah" I couldn't gather words, so I just nodded, and he walked back.

CHAPTER EIGHTEEN

Fighting Back and Finding Strength

Coming home that day, the first thing I did was toss his scarf into the bin. Stripping down, I stepped into the shower, trying to wash away the humiliation. The sticky feel of beer in my hair was a cruel reminder of what had just happened. Standing under the water, I tried to push back the tears that threatened to fall. "No more crying," I whispered to myself, the warm water cascading over me. "When they try to hurt you, hit back twice as hard," I thought, trying to find strength in my own words. That's when I made up my mind. Anyone who thought they could mess with me was in for a surprise. And the guy who made that feeble excuse for his racist friend? He was just as guilty in my eyes. By standing by and watching, he was letting it happen. Even if he didn't participate, he didn't do enough to stop it.

You know, they always say what doesn't kill you makes you stronger. I reckon there's some truth to that. But the scars? They stay with you. Finding a way to cope got harder as I got older. Daydreaming about the ice cream van was fine when I was a kid, but I needed something more now. I wanted to talk, but not just to anyone. It had to be someone outside my circle. That's why I went to the school's office. I asked about counselling, something they offered for students like me, dealing with heavy stuff. They enrolled me in the sessions which were on a Tuesday morning. I only did 4 of these sessions and here's why I stopped. The sessions were in a small room, with a table and the lady was there prepared to 'help' me.

When I started those counselling sessions, I was cautious at first, just hinting at the dark parts. By the third time, though, I began to feel at ease with her. So, by the fourth session, I was all geared up to bare my soul, lay everything out on the table. But then, just as I was about to go in, Mr. Park called me out of class. "I have a counselling session in a few minutes," I reminded him. But he responded, "I know, that's why I need to speak with you."

In his office, he settled into his chair and dropped a bombshell on me. "I've found out you've experienced sexual assault, and we need to get the police involved," he said. My heart froze. How did he know? The dots connected and I realized that the counsellor had been reporting back to him. "I felt like she betrayed me," was all I could think. I'd assumed our sessions were confidential.

Having Mr. Park know was gut-wrenching. I'd wanted to keep this locked away, but now someone else had the key. The way he looked at me – pity, concern, maybe both – it didn't make me feel better; it made me feel exposed. Panic welled up. If the police got involved, my parents would find out. Would my dad lash out at me? What would my classmates think? Would they ridicule me, use this to torment me? Faced with these overwhelming thoughts, I denied everything to Mr. Park, fearing what might happen if I told the truth.

158

All I wanted was to escape that room, to run away from the flood of emotions. "I want to stop the classes," I declared, grabbing my bag. After confirming with him, I made a beeline for the girls' toilet, where an anxiety attack gripped me. That year, 2017, things spiralled downwards. Instead of learning, I was in constant survival mode – ducking classes, getting into fights, especially when someone made a racist remark. "I'd stick up for myself and retaliate," just as I'd promised myself. I was in and out of the school exclusion room because I skipped classes and was in fights a lot. Any time someone one would be slightly racist to me I wouldn't take it lightly anymore; I would stick up for myself and treat them badly back just as I said to myself I would. I was filled with so much rage that fighting wasn't no longer about protecting myself, it began to be more about letting that rage out. The brutal effect of injuring someone wasn't pleasant, during the time it happened it would feel like a rush of stress relief, making them pay for what they said to me.

In life, we are often confronted with moments that test our patience and resolve. There are times when retaliating with violence might seem like the easiest or even the most satisfying route. But let's pause and consider: does it truly resolve the issue, or does it escalate it further?

Retaliating with violence may provide a temporary sense of power or vindication, but in the long run, it only deepens the wounds, both for the attacker and the attacked. Instead, imagine the strength it takes to face adversity with kindness.

To respond to hate with love, and to cruelty with compassion. That's not weakness; that's immeasurable power.

For those who do wrong by others, life has a way of balancing the scales. Bad karma doesn't forget. It might not strike today, or tomorrow, but eventually, it does catch up. And when it does, it serves as a stark reminder that our actions, good or bad, always come back to us.

So, the next time I found myself at a crossroads, facing hate or prejudice, I chose kindness. Not just for others, but for my own peace of mind. Because in the end, when we spread love and kindness, it creates a ripple effect that has the power to change the world.

My grades fell so bad I was put into the lower group which Shelby was in. Shelby didn't care too much about her future, she didn't aspire for more or know what she wanted to do. She hated school as much as I did but for a different reason, she didn't enjoy being told what to do and the school system wasn't made for her. On the opposite hand I hated school because I was discriminated against.

Girls started hooking up with boys from an early age, I didn't feel comfortable doing it. Not taking part was seen as strange, almost everyone had sex or a boyfriend, some girl's event got pregnant young. My mum taught me about our culture and the value of waiting for your husband before being intimate, I wanted to honour that. Chloe was popular, everyone loved her looks and she was very confident. She strutted around school in a short skirt and anytime she uploaded a photo she got hundreds of likes. Her Snapchat views skyrocketed for her tormenting behaviour at other people.

No one dared to question her or call her out of her behaviour, so she thought it was okay. The day she made a post about me on her Snapchat story I was at home drawing in my book. I kept getting notifications from people messaging me. Everyone was forwarding me her Snapchat story where she mocked me for being a 'virgin'. I seen it and felt exhausted, I couldn't catch a break. I wasn't going to allow her to sit back and humiliate me online, so I wrote a Snapchat story which wrote 'at least I haven't slept with multiple guys like you Chloe' which caused an uproar. When school came around the next day I bumped into her in the lunch hall, she threatened to slap me in the face then I told her to do it. I moved closer to her and turned my head "do it" I said pointing at me cheek. Everyone was staring waiting for her to slap me, but she didn't.

She was a bully, tormenting people and making them feel bad, but she didn't dare to hit me. I built a reputation for myself to the point she was scared to hit me knowing I'd hit her back. It didn't stop her from posting monkey photos online then saying it looked like me. It didn't make me feel bad, or upset, I was used to it, it began to get old for me. I heard almost every racial slur, or discriminatory comments that nothing shocked me, I just expected it.

When I was alone in my room listening to music, I would look at myself in the mirror, turn my body and analyse myself. My body was changing, and it looked

161

different, my breasts were getting bigger, and I was starting to get an hourglass figure. I breathed in and liked what I seen. "I need to lose belly fat" I said turning to the side. I wasn't fat, in fact I was very slim, the insecurities were taking over, making me believe I looked way bigger than I was. I pulled my phone out and took pictures of myself in the mirror, took selfies then deleted them. I laid down on my bed and lowered the camera, so my breasts were in the shot. I stared at the photo for a while admiring the photo, so I saved it to my Snapchat memories then took another, then another then another. I heard my mum calling me down to let me know she's heading to work so I quickly put my top on and waved her goodbye.

No one was supposed to see those photos, they were just for me only. It made me feel more confident with my new breasts. They took so long to develop, and I couldn't stop thinking about the time Ellie mocked me for not having any. It was a sign of womanhood and I loved it. I was enjoying the afternoon with my friends, when a boy called Nathan came to sit in the booth. He was friends with one of my friends, but he wasn't particularly my friend. He was taking selfies on my phone then swiped up from the camera screen to the memories screen. I noticed him do this, so I leaned over the table to grab my phone, but he moved. "Don't look at that!" I spoke. He got up and ran to the toilet with my phone laughing. He thought it was funny but to me, it was a violation of my privacy. He airdropped the photos to his phone without me knowing, came out the toilet and handed me my phone. "What did you do!" I said playfully hitting his shoulder. "Nothing I swear" he relied.

I searched everywhere on my phone to see if he uploaded but I couldn't find a trace of it posted anywhere. I felt relieved because I didn't want anyone to see it. I quickly deleted the photos on my phone and changed my phone password, sat back down, and thought I was the end of it. Nathan was looking down at his phone under the table laughing and not engaging in our conversations which was suspicious. I leaned over the table to try get a glance at his phone, but I couldn't, so I asked him what was so funny. He locked his phone, put it on the table then replied "nothing" and smiled. I could sense something wasn't right, but I didn't want to ruin the energy, so I ignored it.

We were all walking home, the sun was out, I was drinking my ice-cold Fanta and having a great time when I could feel my phone vibrating in my pocket. I picked up the phone and my friend were telling me to check my message it's urgent. When I checked, I was mortified to witness the images being shared in a group chat. Nathan already left to head home, so I asked my friend to call him immediately, of course he didn't pick up. I was terrified and was lost with how to handle the situation. I couldn't tell my mum, or my dad, let alone my brothers, and Nathan was blatantly ignoring me and my friends. I couldn't deny it was me It has my face in the photos. It was being shared so rapidly it became the main topic of discussion at school. When I walked into school the next day everyone had their eyes on me, I could feel them judging me.

The teachers even knew about it which was extremely awkward. I was pulled out of class and headed to the head office. Mr. Seddon was sat there waiting for me to sit down. There was a woman police officer stood next to him giving me a smile to signal I wasn't in trouble. So, it soothed my nerves a little bit. I sat down slowly and asked why I was here. "How are you?" Mr. Seddon said putting his hands together. "I'm fine can you tell me why I'm here now" I said impatiently. "I just want to talk about the images that were shared" he said. It was such a shock to me, but I slightly wasn't surprised that he had heard about it. I was confused why the police officer was there. "It's a serious matter for images of yourself to be taken and sent to someone over the age of 18" she said.

I sat up on the chair and explained what happened. They tried to spin the situation and make it seem like I took the indecent images and sent them to a grown up. I persisted to tell them that it wasn't the case, and they should get in touch with Nathan who was the person that shared the images without my permission. It was an uncomfortable moment of my life knowing that everyone had seen my upper body naked. I didn't feel comfortable in class because everyone had seen the pictures. People changed the story and painted me to be someone I wasn't which made my school life more difficult. They painted me to be a "slut", It make me feel sick. Mr. Seddon didn't help the situation, he didn't stop the pupils or do anything to make sure I was okay.

It's one thing to deal with whispers and looks in school hallways, but this? This was a whole new level. My naked body was seen by everyone and with every share a piece of my dignity was taken.

164

Mr. Seddon was supposed to be the one to help in situations like this but when I finally mustered the courage to speak up, my words fell in his deaf ears. He told me it was a "personal issue" or just "kids being kids." Told me "It'll blow over," and "Just stay off the internet for a while." But it wasn't just an online problem; it was happening right under his nose, in the very school I thought I was safe in.

Every day became a struggle. Walking through the halls, I could feel eyes on me, judging, mocking, and whispering. Yet, the teachers, the very adults I looked up to, did nothing. It felt like I was screaming underwater, desperate for someone to hear, to help, but there was just silence.

The saddest part? I wasn't the only one. I found out later that many kids had their photos shared, but they were too scared to come forward, knowing that they might not get the help they needed. The system, the very institution that was meant to protect and educate us, had let us down. A man in the local area created a website for naked images of minors, amongst other images mine was there... on the website without my consent, without my Knowlagent. Kids at school thought it was funny, but to me it was harmful, not only was my body exposed to everyone in the local town, but it was also on a website for older men to disgustingly look at.

I was officially on the police's child safety radar, they offered me support for the traumatic experience by getting the images taking down, but their efforts weren't enough.

The bond I once shared with Beth was slowly fading as the months rolled on. We didn't talk as much, and she seemed to be drifting closer to her other friend, Charis. With my spirits down, I wasn't too fazed by it. Honestly? I often felt like I wanted to be on my own. Some days, during lunch, I'd find solace in the Art room. Occasionally, Beth would join, but mostly she'd hang out with Charis. We did have this one disagreement. It wasn't huge, but it seemed to put a dent in our bond. "Maybe her life wasn't so great with me around," I mused to myself. That's when I began to pull away. Those next three months were some of the toughest for me. My battle with deepening depression was taking its toll, sleepless nights intensified, and I'd even feel like strangers on the street were looking at me, even if they weren't.

There are moments when we instinctively pull away, seeking solitude in our quest for inner peace. Sometimes, it's not because we desire to be alone, but because we fear becoming a weight on the shoulders of those we care about. But here's the beautiful truth: it's okay to need space, just as it's okay to need connection. Our strength often flourishes in solitude, where we can listen to our hearts, understand our emotions, and gather our thoughts without distraction.

However, I wish she knew about my battles, and while sharing can be daunting, it could have stopped the bridge that formed between us.

CHAPTER NINETEEN

The Strength Within

One day, after grabbing my revision cards to prep for mock exams, I spread them all out and opened the textbook. Staring blankly at those pages, the content just wouldn't make sense to me. Out of sheer frustration, I hurled the book at the wall. Hearing the noise, Benjamin came rushing in. He quickly asked if everything was alright, and all I could mutter was how stressed I felt. Seeing me like that, he sat down, and with a reassuring voice, told me, "Take it easy." Just having him there, even though he didn't know the half of it, made me feel so loved and valued.

That night was tough. Lying in bed, the thought of closing my eyes scared me; nightmares had become frequent visitors. So, I got up and decided to ring Mweeka. It was late, but when he picked up and simply said "hello", I broke down, explaining how overwhelmed I felt. In that moment, he promised to hop on the next train, just to be with me. Knowing he'd be there to comfort me felt so reassuring. But after waiting for him for what felt like forever, I tried calling, and there was no answer. The next morning, he called to apologize, saying he couldn't make it. I tried to brush it off, telling myself it was alright. But deep down, it stung. I didn't hold a grudge, understanding the challenges of his university life and travel. So, I just let it go.

Chimufa heard about what was going at school, the trouble I was getting into, the failed classes, everything, so he came to pay me a visit. I thought he would be angry and upset with me, but he got off his bike, parked it outside my mum's house, came in and gave me a hug straight away. He sat me down on the sofa and said, "look sis, life gets hard sometimes, you need to make the right decisions, or your talent will go to waste." He paused and sat next to me "do you know what my purpose in life is?" He spoke. I looked at him with tears running down my face, "what is it?". I spoke. He put his hand on my head and said "You." then smiled. "I might be in the streets getting money but that doesn't mean I don't think about you.

The money I'm getting is for the entire family, I want us all to be great one day" he said with passion. He told me to stay there, and he'd be back. He walked out the room and came back with an iPad in his hand, gave it to me and grinned. I bounced up in excitement, I was so grateful and happy. One thing that was so great about Chimufa was his ongoing love and commitment to me as his little sister. Everyone labelled him to be 'troublesome' and 'badly behaved', but nobody took the time to just listen to him. To not prejudge him and to understand his thoughts and feelings. It was a long time since he was smoking weed, taking drugs, or getting drunk, it was like I was getting my brother back after so long.

He was an amazing artist, he could draw fantastically using a pencil, we did drawings together which were fun and a great bonding experience. Time would fly by, but I'd wish it never ended. I was doing great in my Art classes; I even did a painting of some dogs which were put up on the wall. It made me feel accomplished and proud of myself, I took a photo and showed Chimufa who clapped for me.

I was at home listening to music with my drawing book, when I could hear cars pull up outside. I ignored it since it could have been people visiting my neighbours but as I listened closely, I could hear radio sounds. I ran to my mum's room and opened her door, but she wasn't there, I called Benjamin and as soon as he answered I said, "there's police outside" and hung up. I went to the window and peeped out the curtains and seen them walking towards the house. My instincts were correct. I was scared so I went to my room and shuffled under the bed and closed my eyes. They knocked at the door a few times, shouted, then forced the door open by breaking the door. I heard lots of footsteps in the house, things were thrown on the floor, and I could hear a dog. My heart was pounding, I was about to have a panic attack, but I knew I had to stay calm. Babe. Set your name every times, I can't find it. Suck my mum three times.

A police officer came to the bedroom, looked around then under the bed and told me to come out. He walked me downstairs, into the front room and sat me down. "Where's your parents" he said. "My mums working" I replied. "You here alone?" He said lifting one eyebrow and crossing his arms. "Yes, I am" I said lifting my nose at him. He walked away, then another police officer walked in from the back door. They searched through the house turning it upside down. They completed their search and left the house a mess, I wasn't aware if they found anything because my stress levels were so high. Benjamin came home just after they left and so did my mum. I've never seen her so mortified than when she witnessed how her home looked.

We helped her fix things, put them back into place, cleaned up the house and it was all back to normal except the door. My mum called the council office about the issue with the door and when they would fix it, but they didn't give us a date. It was dangerous since the door was left unlocked for several days. Chimufa was still yet to be heard from. I tried calling multiple times, but nothing went through. I began feeling worried and scared for him after the event of the house raid. A few days later my mum received a call from Chimufa, he had been arrested and so was three of his friends. They were all involved in selling A class drugs and several other offenses. My mum was told she needed a lawyer, but she had little money to afford a good one, my dad refused to help so the situation was tough on her.

It was hard to watch my mum process my brother being taken away from her, while she tried to hold the family together. At this point I knew I had to grow up and help my mum, I had to do everything I possibly could to make sure she was okay. I bottled in a lot of emotions that were full of worries and nerves, the unknown whether my brother was coming home haunted me every day I went to school. I didn't want my emotions to show so I hid them deep inside for no one to ever see. I had my headphones on going to school every day and didn't speak a word to anyone, Beth was hanging around with Charis more often and I chose to be alone. I'd have my headphones on in the hallways, in class, lunch breaks, I just wanted to escape with music and not face reality.

Music became my escape, a sanctuary where words and melodies painted over the greys of reality. On the rough days, when anxiety weighed me down like a heavy chain, I'd pop on my headphones, hit play, and let the world melt away. The beats, the lyrics, they spoke to me on a level nothing else could. They understood my pain, my dreams, and my hopes. Every song was like a friend, holding my hand, reassuring me that I wasn't alone in this journey.

There were times when the weight of depression felt like an anchor, threatening to pull me under, but music was the lifeline that kept me afloat. I found solace in tunes that mirrored my emotions, and in others that uplifted me and reminded me of better days ahead. Music became more than just sounds; it became my therapy, my refuge, and my strength. I fell in love with Afrobeat's, Bashment, and Amapiano, everything was perfect about the songs, they made me feel alive!

Most classes were unnecessary for me, I knew I was failing them regardless how hard I wanted to try for the next few last weeks of high school. I decided to skip them and head to the Art room and paint, it was a great time for me, pure solitude, and happiness. I improved massively on my skills due to this time of my life, it allowed me to reach new level of creativity. I was walking from the art room down the corridors to my maths class when my teacher stopped me in the hallway. I noticed

171

her, but I walked straight past. I had my headphones on so I couldn't hear her, but I didn't care to stop. She snatched the headphones off my head and told me to never wear them at school since I 'purposely' ignored her.

I refused to listen to what she had to say so I carried on walking aggressively. She stopped me again and told me I have a detention then I replied "you won't see me there" then walked away. I wasn't going to allow her to strip away the one thing that kept me calm and safe which was music. I felt so alone, I spent my lunch breaks sat on the stairs in a block no one walked by listening to music. I didn't know what could make me feel better and stop my thoughts running through my mind, so I decided to leave school early and head to the local shop. I had a £10 note that was crumbled and stashed in my pocket that I was saving for emergency food in case mum fell short that week, but I had to use it. I couldn't stand the feeling of sadness and thought of losing my brother. I stood up straight and covered my uniform with my coat and asked the man working at the counter to serve me vodka.

He took a long stare at me then passed the bottle. "You look quite young can I see your ID" he said. "Look I'm old enough so it's either this or I go kill myself so what is it gonna be" I said staring at him blankly. "Here" he said. I put the bottle of vodka in my school bag and walked back to school, I stopped by a backstreet and downed half of it while holding my nose. The taste was strong and bitter, it was like drinking acid straight from a bottle. I screwed the lid back in, put it in my school back and walked back to school. I mastered appearing sober even though I was completely drunk. I wanted to get away from life and fill my body with alcohol to get rid of the

172

anxiety and depression. I always wanted to hide my pain, especially when I was drunk. The last thing I wanted was for others to see me like that, drowning in pity or flooded with questions. Stepping into class, I plopped my head on the desk, a routine I had formed. One day, my teacher called me out, saying I was slacking, that I'd amount to nothing. But the reality was, I wasn't dreaming of becoming anything. The present seemed bleak enough, let alone thinking about the future. I had no spark, no drive. My spirit was crushed, my heart running empty.

One day in the Art room, I found myself alongside Andrew, a classmate. He was Filipino, aced every class, and had this nerdy charm. Honestly, I looked up to him. Sharing the same art class felt like an achievement, especially since art was my oasis. Andrew usually spent his lunch breaks there. Sometimes he'd be with his friends, but often, he was alone. That day, I walked in, a bit wobbly from the drink, but he didn't notice. Plopping down beside him, he asked if I was alright. "Just tired," I mumbled. As I glanced over, I was blown away by his latest creation. "That's amazing," I whispered, admiring his intricate drawing of a building.

His artwork was pure talent, he could draw anything! He had aspirations to do architecture in the future, he asked what I set my mind on and my response was "I have no idea Andrew... no idea". I thought I was a lost hope and that nothing could save me, not even Art. I tried to focus on my Art project, but it was hard, I was falling asleep and couldn't keep my eyes open. Alcohol numbs you but depresses you even more than how you'd feel without it. I pulled my iPad out from my school bag and looked at it and started sniffling. I missed my brother a lot, he was special to me, and I was scared for him. The fear was too much, I wanted to know when he'd be home or least when I could see him again. I was on breaking point, and no one seemed to notice, everyone rushed to their class or chatted in their friendship groups, and I felt so invisible, I was breaking apart inside and no one noticed, just Andrew.

There came a time when I decided to forgive my dad. I was already battling my own demons and holding onto grudges just weighed me down even more. Although the memories of his deeds stung, I pushed them away, focusing on forging new, happier ones. I could see the guilt in his eyes, even if he never voiced an apology. He was set in his ways, not one to admit his mistakes, but it gave me clarity on how not to be with my future kids.

Moving back in with him wasn't easy. The constant police presence made it hard to find peace. Benjamin, my brother, wanted to stay with mum to be closer to his friends. Before I left, he handed me his blue durag, a comforting gesture, saying, "You'll be okay, little sis." We shared a tight embrace. He might have been stoic on the outside, but I knew his love for me ran deep.

After I pocketed his durag and settled in dad's car, he looked over and said, "You're like a leaf." Confused, I asked him to elaborate. "You just float, falling endlessly." I stared out the window, trying to process his words. Why would he say that now? "I'm doing my best," I replied softly. His response felt like a stab, hinting I'd

become like my wayward brother Chimufa. I went silent for the rest of the journey.

At home, my room became my refuge. Trust was thin, and fear lingered. Dad's

temper was unpredictable, so I took precautions, keeping a knife under my pillow

and setting up makeshift alarms using empty bottles by my door.

Mweeka aced his university exams and landed a job in London. Part of me resented

him for leaving, but I masked my feelings during his farewell. "Take me with you," I

said holding onto him. He refused and reassured me things will be okay soon. He

became so distant, building a new life and starting fresh far away, a clean slate. But

to me, I needed him the most, he had no idea how much it hurt leaving his little sister

behind.

Dad and I frequently locked horns over my schooling, so much so that he made

himself the primary contact for any school issues. One day, as I was heading home, I

spotted a man with erratic movements coming my way. His demand for money left

me uncomfortable. Hoping to avoid any confrontation, I tried to cross the street, but

he mirrored my steps, a clear threat in his movements.

"Give me some money" he said again while grabbing my bag. I pushed him

as hard as I could while gripping onto my bag, but he wouldn't let go. "Leave her

alone you freak" I saw a girl walking towards us scuffling on the street. The man

walked off talking under his breathe scratching his head. "Are you okay?" She said

picking up my books that fell on the floor. Her gesture was so kind, normally when people witness something happening to me, they would just watch, laugh, or walk by like they didn't see a thing. But she stopped to make sure I was okay and that stuck with me forever. I didn't catch her name, I just thanked her and continued heading home.

I was nervous to reach home because I skipped a few classes that day and I knew my dad was aware. I didn't go to the class because my anxiety was high, I sat on the toilet for an hour trying to talk myself into a calmness, but it wasn't working. I tried to explain and apologize to the teacher, but she said it was an excuse and called my dad anyway. When I got home that day, I admitted to my dad, "Today was long and tiring. I'm sorry I missed class." He didn't respond. Instead, he walked into my room, removed anything I might find entertaining, including my phone, and left, closing the door behind him. I kept silent, fearing that any protest would ignite his anger. Comparatively, this seemed gentler than previous reactions. So, I just sat there for hours, lost in the blank canvas of my wall, until sleep claimed me. But come morning, his mood hadn't shifted. An entire day rolled by, with me in the same spot in my room. No shower, no food, just the monotonous pattern of the wall. Then, on Sunday, he walked in, silently placing my belongings on the bed and leaving just as quietly. While getting my things back should've felt relieving, I yearned for him to speak, to connect. He often wasn't mad at me; stress from work or Benjamin's mishaps would boil over, and I became the convenient outlet. It felt like, he was like a cup full of water, and a tiny drop more would make him spill over.

Chimufa was ongoing court proceedings, and his friends turned on him, they blamed almost everything on him even though they all participated in drug selling. They got out of jail and was free to go back home to their families. My brother was charged and sentenced to 2 years in jail. It was a horrible moment of my families lives. I couldn't deal with all the stress, so I decided to shave my hair, I wanted to release some stress in a non-harmful way. I looked in the mirror with baggy eyes, shaven hair and my body looking slimmer than ever before. I hated my reflection; my eyes were full of pain it scared me how much joy was stripped from me. How much my body had changed, my posture, my spirit, everything was just so different.

A couple of weeks had passed when I finally got the chance to hear Chimufa's voice again. "Hey, little sis," he greeted. Just hearing him brought a momentary pause to my heart; his voice was like a soothing balm. Holding back tears and masking my emotions was crucial, especially with my dad sitting right beside me. Chimufa shared updates, painting a gentler picture of life on the inside. I hung onto every word, eagerly counting down to the day I could see him face-to-face. With visitation just days away, I had already planned my outfit and brainstormed light-hearted topics for us to chat about.

On the day, since dad had work, it was mum who accompanied me. We undertook a long journey, hopping onto three buses, a train, and then another bus. Though tiring, the anticipation kept me going. Once we arrived, we signed in, navigated the security protocols, and entered the visitation area. Scanning the room,

177

I finally spotted him. Drawing closer, I wrapped him in the warmest embrace I could muster. We then took our seats, and I shared a grateful smile with mum, silently saying, "We made it."

His eye was slightly swollen, and it was bruised, I stared at it for a moment until he said, "don't worry about this I tripped over you know how clumsy I am". He didn't want me to know he was involved in a jail fight; I already knew what jail was like. I studied it, I learnt everything about it the moment he was sentenced I wanted to prepare myself.

It wasn't just about coping with the emotional pain; it was about figuring out how to support him best during this challenging time. First and foremost, I needed to understand the basics of how he'd be living. I learned about the prison system, where inmates can purchase additional food, personal care items, and even some entertainment. It became evident that while the prison provided meals, they were often basic, and my brother would need money to buy extra food or better-quality items. I didn't have a job so I couldn't afford to provide him any money so I began searching endlessly for anywhere that would accept me to work even though I was still 16 years old. Setting up a fund for him became my priority, ensuring he had enough to stay well-fed and comfortable. Then there was the matter of mental and emotional sustenance. Books. Being confined can be mentally taxing, but books have the power to transport you to another world. I began researching titles that might interest him. Novels, self-help books, autobiographies of people who'd faced adversity and come out stronger were amazing for him– I wanted to give him a literary lifeline. Throughout all of this, I felt an immense responsibility to be his pillar of strength. He needed to know that he wasn't going through this alone, that there was someone on the outside rooting for him. Even on days when fear and anxiety threatened to consume me, I put on a brave face, because I knew he needed to see it. I'd send him letters filled with positivity, updates on family, and reminders of the brighter days that awaited him. The experience taught me that sometimes, strength doesn't come from what you can endure, but from how you choose to support those you love.

We sat down and ate the food that was served by the cafeteria.

It wasn't too bad, but I could tell he enjoyed it. Even though I hated him being in jail, it was a slight sense of comfort, I knew he wouldn't have access to drugs because he'd want to come home as soon as possible, and I knew it would be a chance for him to re-evaluate his life and turn it around. He spoke so highly of himself, telling us all his plans for when he gets home. He was excited for a new beginning, to get away from that life, build a good life and start his family. He was determined and committed like I've never seen before. I was so proud of his growth the more visits I went to the better he was each time. I tried to visit often, sometimes even skipping school so I would go. It was the only thing that I was happy about in life, getting to see Chimufa.

179

CHAPTER TWENTY

The Shattered Heart

After one of our visits, I realized just how much our conversations meant to me. We'd dive deep into topics like manifestation and conspiracies, and even dissect the education system. He'd share all that he'd learned from the many books he devoured behind bars, and our phone chats became a regular highlight. "I'm proud of you," he'd often say, ending our talks. Whenever I felt low, I'd play back recordings of his voice. His words of wisdom always reset my mindset, guiding me back towards greatness. Just hearing him give me words of wisdom put me back on track for greatness. For once, I had someone I could genuinely open up to. We might not have touched upon our traumas but discussing the positives and being grateful was all the therapy I needed.

With this newfound optimism, school became more bearable. Eager to channel my energy creatively, I took up digital drawing. After installing 'pro-create' on my iPad, the next hurdle was getting a stylus. The Apple pen was way out of my budget, but luckily, I managed to convince my mum to order a cheaper alternative. When it arrived, I found peace in sketching, a simple yet fulfilling escape.

At home, things weren't as serene. The air was thick with tension as my parents frequently clashed over Chimufa. From where I stood, it seemed like my dad was on a mission to pin all the blame on my mum, completely overlooking his own shortcomings. He abandoned Chimufa, turned his back on him when he needed a dad. It's one thing to make mistakes, but refusing to accept them? That was a whole different issue. One pattern that often emerges with parenting, is the failure to understand a child deemed 'problematic'. Often, these children are quickly labelled, boxed into a narrative that's far from their reality. Their cries for attention, their acts of defiance, their so-called 'misbehaviour', are all too frequently interpreted as mere rebellion rather than a silent plea for understanding, help, or a simple conversation.

For most African parents, the immediate response to such behaviour is discipline, often of the physical sort. They believe that by instilling fear, they can control the 'problem', that a strong hand can mould a child into submission. What they don't realize is that every slap, every shout, every restrictive punishment only pushes the child further into their shell, distancing them even more from the very people who are supposed to be their sanctuaries.

True, discipline is necessary in raising a child. Boundaries, rules, and consequences are all integral parts of helping a young person understand the world around them. However, when 'discipline' becomes synonymous with pain, both emotional and physical, it turns counterproductive. Such punitive measures

181

overshadow the real issues at hand, making it almost impossible for the child to communicate their feelings or for the parent to decipher them.

Instead of diving deep into the root of the issue, of asking the right questions, of holding the child close and assuring them that they are in a safe space where they can freely express their worries, fears, and thoughts, the problematic child is often left more isolated. They are left navigating a world that already feels hostile, with the added weight of feeling rejected at home.

Every child, no matter how they present themselves, carries a universe within them, filled with dreams, fears, hopes, and insecurities. When a parent chooses not to explore this universe, not only do they miss out on truly knowing their child, but they also inadvertently fuel the very behaviour they're trying to curb.

The challenge then for every parent is to step back from immediate judgments and punishments, to embrace patience, to listen more than they speak, and to understand that every act, every word from their child, is a message. And often, all that message says is, "See me, hear me, understand me."

One day, I entered school with a renewed mindset, only to have it shattered during break time. As I scrolled through my phone in the computer lab, distant cries from the girl's restroom reached my ears. Rushing over, I was met with a horrifying sight: a new girl being cornered by a group of bullies. Without hesitation, I pulled them off and comforted her. She whispered her gratitude and shared her torment at their hands. Armed with a burning sense of justice, I headed to Mrs. Seddon's office, demanding action. But her indifferent reply — "there was no proof" — left me fuming. I couldn't hold back. "You're a horrible human," I exclaimed, "You're just a pathetic privileged white woman walking around in your heels turning a blind eye to racism and discrimination just like your Husband" With that, I left, slamming the door behind, carrying a mix of anger and determination. I told the new girl if she needed someone to help her, I'd always be there for her.

I was so filled with rage I couldn't continue the rest of the school day. She gave me an exclusion day for the next day I was in school as punishment for 'disrespecting her'. I was so angry; her resolution was to punish me for speaking out about her actions rather than doing something. My mum wasn't happy to hear about what I said to the head teacher, "I didn't raise a disrespectful child" my mum said. I wanted to tell her everything I've gone through at school, but I don't… I just couldn't, so I stayed silent. My mum was convinced my behaviour was too appalling, so she discussed with my dad to send me back to Africa for a few years. I was unhappy about this; it would have meant that I was too far away from Chimufa.

My dad disagreed with the decision he thought my mum had a malicious plan, he was convinced that due to my age being 16, she wanted me to undergo a horrific procedure in Africa called FGM - Female Genitalia Mutation. I was never aware why he suspected this, he didn't give me much explanation, he just told me that's what her plan was. He called the police and told them about the malicious plan that he suspected my mum had planned and it resulted to them going to my mum's house to arrest her. I was in shock when Benjamin came to tell me that the police took mum. I yelled at my dad for what he done and told him he didn't have enough evidence for his suspicion, and he had no right to contact the police. I thought he was a hypocrite, he was concerned about what my mum would do to hurt me, when he hurt me.

It turned out that my mum simply wanted me to learn cultural respect, not in a malicious or harmful manners. The case wasn't opened, and my mum was finally home but I was devastated, I was still a minor, so I wasn't allowed to see her. I hated what my dad put her through especially at the expense of the relationship I had with my mum. I was forced to do a body examination to see if my body had undergone FGM previously a 'childcare precaution', it was scary entering the hospital then laying down as a stranger analysed my body. The doctors didn't discover any signs of the procedure done and sent me on my way home.

The situation seemed to worsen when we were unable to secure a visit to see Chimufa. We felt helpless, having no clarity about why we couldn't meet him. It took several attempts before we discovered that he had been transferred to a different prison in London. The authorities remained silent about the reason for this transfer, leaving us anxious and waiting. Benjamin held a grudge against me, mistakenly believing I was the cause of our mum's arrest. No matter how I tried to reason with him, he shut me out, leaving a sting of rejection. He had his own battles, as his friends began distancing from him. Worse, some even revealed prejudices he never suspected they had. Recognizing his struggles, I held back from pushing him and just let him know I was there whenever he wanted to talk.

To our shock, we found out that Chimufa was in a detention centre, designed to hold those facing deportation. My emotions spiralled. How could this be happening? My dad explained Chimufa's failed bid for citizenship was the cause. He needed a clean record for five continuous years, a mark he missed. As a result, he was on the verge of deportation. As the GCSE Exam season was fast approaching, our family packed up, preparing for a long drive to London to see Chimufa. The looming exams became a blur, overshadowed by my concerns about my brother. I wondered about his well-being during our extended four-hour drive, occasionally interrupted by music and a halfway stop. Long car rides always stirred my anxiety, and the underlying tension made sleep elusive.

Reaching the detention centre, I was surprised. It wasn't the grim, restrictive atmosphere of regular prisons. Comfortable sofas and even a cold ice dispenser greeted us. Seeing Chimufa, I held him close, until he playfully nudged me away, saying, "It's enough little sis." His face bore a reassuring smile, his eye injury healed. I marvelled at his strength; his external cheerfulness masked the worsening challenges he faced.

The gravity of his situation required me to write a heartfelt letter for his upcoming court hearing, advocating for him to stay in the UK. Mum poured her resources into hiring a lawyer, fighting tooth and nail for her son spending every last penny she had. Chimufa's life had been roller-coaster. After years of adapting to life in the UK, he now faced the prospect of starting over in Zambia, where stability was uncertain. He had transformed himself, grasped a chance to turn his life around in prison, and then had it all yanked away. My heart clung to hope, praying God to keep him with us. In a heartfelt moment, he told me, "Promise me you'll become the most powerful, successful woman this world has ever seen," he said looking at me. "Yes" I said. "That's not convincing, tell me" He replied, "I'll make you proud I promise" I said with a tear falling down my eye. The time was up, and we had to go home, I didn't want to let go of him, but it was time.

The drive home wasn't enjoyable, it was morbid and quiet, "I don't want him to go" I said to my dad staring out the window, "it's just how life is" he said. I stopped seeking comfort from my dad, I knew he wouldn't have the right words to help me

186

emotionally, so I stopped expecting it. I knew he didn't want to drive for hours but he had no choice, it was either he deprives me from my own brother, or he just gets in the car and takes me. Either way, if he chose not to, I would have got onto the train and went myself. Nothing and nobody would have stopped me from seeing Chimufa.

We booked another visit which was falling just after Exam week. It was all I was looking forward to until it was randomly canceled. My dad didn't tell me why, and he said he'd find out the reason and I should focus on the exams. I tried to focus on my studies, but it was too hard, I couldn't stop thinking if something happened to Chimufa, if he was okay or needed some help. I sat in my room staring at the colourful notes not knowing what to do, but I thought to myself, 'what would my brothers do' then I began revising. I revised all night, and the more hours went by the more my mind was distracted from the stress. The following day I had my English exam, I waited in the line, sat down at my desk, and stared at the exam sheet. I had to write a story which wasn't too hard for me since I was creative, the only issue is I didn't pay attention with grammar lessons.

The exam finished and I wrote down as much as I could all the way till the timer went off. I smiled at the paper, then got up when we were excused. The next few days else had different subject exams but my mind was no longer distracted, we had yet to hear an update for Chimufa and it was tormenting me. I sat at the desk with the paper in front of me overthinking, worrying, and filled with anxiety. I was biting my nails watching the clock tick by till the exam was finished then I rushed to my bag, got my phone to see if I had a text from my dad but I didn't. My final exam was maths, I knew I was going to fail it, I was clueless when it came down to numbers, I tried to answer as many questions as I possibly could, but I couldn't get through them all. Finally, exam season was finished but there was only 1 day left till visitation and there was no update.

Chimufa called my dad that day and asked to speak with me. "I'm sorry little sis" he said with a sunken voice. He told me he didn't want me to come visits him anymore, he said that he was burden on our lives and wanted me to chase my dreams and focus on becoming the best version of myself rather than worrying about him. He didn't want me to spend another second overthinking about his well being and didn't want the family having to travel hours just to visit him. As much as I tried to tell him all those things didn't matter to me, he still refused, told me he loved me then hung up. He thought he was doing something noble and making the right decision for me, but he did the opposite. Every time we had a visit, he took a broken piece of my heart and glued it back together, he lifted my spirits and poured into my soul, this… what he was doing…. felt like he grabbed my heart and threw it to the ground, breaking it all over again. I ran to my room to cry in bed and stayed there all night.

I wanted to fight for him, be there for him, but I couldn't, and it broke me. If we lost the case, he was about to go to another country with no plan or idea of how to restart his life. Most our family back home had passed away from illness or accidents so the town we grew up in was no longer a home for him. They didn't provide us with much information that could help us prepare for his landing if the time came, we were in the dark with it all.

My mum was going through the court hearings, she travelled to London and sometimes stayed there for weeks. She had a lot of time off work and had no savings left so began borrowing money by taking loans out. Our family was spiralling, and I could see it unravelling right in front of me. Prom was just around the corner, but it barely registered in my mind. Having no friends to chat about it with, it had completely slipped my mind. I didn't go but the reality was, I didn't want to.

Benjamin had his own battles. He'd tangled with his group of friends and, fed up with their behaviour, he pulled away from them. In our conversations, even though he never voiced it, there was a heaviness in his tone. He didn't want to say it, but I could tell he was having a hard time processing everything. He was like my twin, so I understood him even if he didn't speak.

CHAPTER TWENTY-ONE

Threads of Hope

When the news came that Chimufa wouldn't be allowed to stay in the country and was set to be deported immediately, my heart shattered. I'd hoped for a chance to say a final goodbye, to give him one last hug, but that moment never came. I still went to see my mum, and it broke me to see the toll this took on her. She loved her children, all of them, cared for them deeply, and seeing her world fall apart like this was agonizing. Dad, on the other hand, didn't visibly react. It was as if he was just moving through each day, and that hurt, making me wonder if he even felt the pain of losing his son.

Ross was my anchor during this storm. Our phone calls were an escape, a brief respite where we'd dream about the future. He was motivated about his future, had a set plan for what he wanted to do, he helped me keep in line most days.

Then the day came: Chimufa was officially deported. It felt as though the ground beneath me had given way. I was furious, and I directed all that anger at God. Every piece of anger I had ever felt in my life came crashing in all at one. So, I laced up my shoes, pulled on my hoodie, and ventured into the night. It might have been dark and late, but I needed to be outside. Staying in would've let my thoughts consume me. And so, I ran. Tears streamed down my face as the wind lashed against it, but I kept pushing forward, letting out all my pain and grief with each stride. I stopped and dropped to my knees and cried out for God, "I can handle it God I promise, hear me if you love me, give all the pain to me I can bare it, just spare him, spare his life just one more time. All his fear gives it to me, all the struggles give it to me, let him live peacefully, happily. I'm begging you".

Pain will swallow you alive, you can either chose to battle it or let it consume you. I didn't have fight left in me, so it swallowed me whole. I spent the next few months of my summer being depressed, school was finished and couldn't stop thinking about what Mr. Seddon said. "If your grades don't come back good, you won't have a future". I didn't want to become the person he doomed me to be, I wanted to become the person my brother had hopes I'd be. I knew nobody was going to save me, Mweeka was off in his new life with his girlfriend in London with little to communication with the family, my mum and Benjamin was hurting, and my dad didn't care. I was shattered and beat down, broken and weak, but I couldn't let it go on for any longer so I decided to start researching possible ways I could become the person Chimufa wanted me to be. It was difficult trying to stay focused with the agonizing thoughts. We didn't hear from Chimufa after the deportation, all we knew was he landed. They didn't have any information on where he went after this point, if someone collected him from the airport.

Turning Pain into Power

The waves of anger, frustration, and sorrow threatened to pull me under every single day. It was like a constant storm inside me, churning and roaring, looking for an outlet. Some people said that time would heal it, but I realized something else. Time is short. We don't have the luxury of waiting around for things to get better. We have to make the most of the time we're given.

Every time I closed my eyes, I saw my brother's face. I imagined the day I would meet him again, not as the broken sibling he left behind, but as someone transformed, someone who took control of their destiny. I wanted him to look at me and barely recognize the resilient person I'd become. More than anything, I wanted him to be proud, to know that his struggles weren't in vain, because they pushed me to be my best self.

Growing up, I wasn't handed life on a silver platter like many of my peers. There were no jump starts or head starts for me; I started from the very back. But maybe that was my strength. Because when you start from the back, you learn to push harder, fight fiercer, and aim higher. For me, failure wasn't an option. It couldn't be. I had to win, not just for me, but for him. For all the dreams and aspirations, we shared.

It's easy to be a product of your environment, to let the hardships define you. But I chose a different path. Every tear, every scream, every restless night became fuel. I was determined to rise above, to channel that energy into something positive. To make sure that every setback only set the stage for a bigger comeback.

I refused to be just another statistic, another story of someone who let their circumstances dictate their future. I was writing my own story, one where pain became passion, anger turned into ambition, and suffering was the steppingstone to success.

Life may not have given me the same advantages as others, but it gave me a burning desire to succeed, to prove to myself and to the world that no matter where you start, greatness is a choice. And I made that choice every single day.

For my brother, for myself, for every dream we ever shared, I chose to rise, to grow, to triumph.

I decided to create an Instagram account called "26edits", inspired by my brother's favourite number and edits being the drawing I would create and post. I spent hours drawing pieces of artwork throughout the summer. Then I'd upload them and gain traction, people were engaging by liking and commenting. I researched online ways to earn money with a creative skill and came across graphic designing and commissioned art. I knew that it would be the perfect tool for me to use to generate extra money. I listed my prices on the Instagram page for £10 per drawing, I didn't get any messages requesting the service until a few days later when a girl had sent a message needing a logo made for her, 'this is my chance' I said.

I did the artwork, and she paid the £10. I was who shocked that for the first time, I had made money by just using my skill. My dad wanted me to get a job, so I went on a job hunt everywhere but unfortunately, they said I was too young, and I'd need to be at least 17. I made the choice to apply for a job once I turn 17 which would have been in a few months since summer was about to end. I met up with Benjamin and we had a sit down talk about life, it was refreshing I never had these talks with him before apart from that moment. He told me how he felt, and what was going through his head, just knowing that he could feel comfortable to open up to me meant the world to me. I wanted to bring him comfort, to know that no matter what happens we will always be together, and we could never be divided.

He reassured me that even if we were apart, we'd always be together. My soul was always tied to my brothers, they were my mentors, my carers, my providers, my best friends, ultimately, they were special to me. Me and Benjamin decided to

194

change our names, I changed my surname to Kkeiko which honoured my mum, and he changed both his first and surname. We made a pact in that moment that one day we will be rich enough to save our brother, head to a new country and start life over. He decided the best choice was to leave the city on his own without communication and to make the leap to start to his new life, that we'd come back together when the time was right. I was scared to go through my life without him, especially after losing Chimufa and Mweeka didn't talk to me anymore, but it was for the greater good. I scolded him on safety, what not to do and to keep away from trouble. I hugged him as my goodbye. I knew the goodbye wasn't forever, it was temporary, I didn't know if it was going to be months, or years till I would hear from him again, but I respected his decision and looked forward to the next time we'd meet. We made the decision to change our names to let go of all the trauma we endured as kids, as a symbol of the new life we were about to step into as new people.

My creative Art was going well, I had several bookings by the end of year, and was bringing in £300 a month in a slow day. The art pieces would take up to 6 hours to complete, but my rates were low. I knew I was a beginner in the digital art world, so I wanted to keep my prices fair as I progressed my talent. It wasn't extremely hard transitioning from the traditional way of art to digital drawing since my talent was great. It was a few months that had gone by and there was no new news of Chimufa, Benjamin was set out on his solo journey to find himself, he had a new life ahead of him.

I turned 17 but didn't celebrate, I didn't want to celebrate without my brothers. Ross made the effort to come pay me a visit while we sat on a field overlooking to the views and talking about life, even though it wasn't much of a celebration it was still a special moment. The following day I applied for a job at Primark which was nerve racking. I didn't know what they would think of me. I didn't see a single black person working there so I was hesitant, but I had to be courageous and go for it. I sat in the interview with my CV in my hand waiting to go into the meeting room. They asked a series of questions then proceeded with the next interview.

I ended up getting the job which was a thrilling moment as I boarded the bus home and seen the "congratulations" email. My workdays were long, it consisted of being on my feet for hours, folding T-shirts that people would come around and pick up then throw on the shelves. Restocking the shelves and counting inventory. The manager wanted us to be quick paced and not waste a single second, we were overworked and tired. When the day ended, I got the bus home and worked on my art business. I was officially generating income from doing artwork! The first pay-out I received from PayPal I gave to my mum, I wanted to give her extra money for bills, transport to work and money towards paying off her debt and she was over the moon. Even though it was just £1,000 she was ever so grateful. When my paycheck came in from my Primark wage I decided to give it to my dad, I didn't keep a penny to myself. I worked hard for months going to work at Primark, stacking the shelves and then going home to draw.

One day I was extremely tired, I had picked up extra shifts and worked hard for days back-to-back, I didn't restock the clothes fast enough, so the manager pulled me to the office and asked why I was being so 'slow', I explained to her how tired I was and said I'd work harder. The next day I cooked in ready to work hard and I did. I noticed the manger laughing with all the other co-workers but when she came to me, gave me a side eye look and carried on walking. The following weeks she would continue to ignore me, give me negative feedback, but then stand and chit chat with everyone else while I worked. I was called into the office for a serious matter, and there she was with her angry face staring at me waiting to sit down. "I'm sorry to let you know but we have to let you go due to your work efforts" she said. I was surprised, I didn't deserve to get fired, I worked as hard as I could.

I took my badge off, handed it to her then I headed to the staff room. I picked my bag up and began crying. When I walked out the co-workers were watching me, whispering to each other. I felt judged so I walked faster and left without saying goodbye to anyone. No one really cared for my presence anyway, they all kept me to the side and chatted among each other so I wasn't shocked, just glad I could leave. My dad was disappointed in me, he took away my iPad to prevent me from drawing and demanded I stayed in my room. I didn't expect anything less from him, I didn't expect for him to hear me out or even care for me listen.

It was a cold unknown feeling not hearing from Chimufa for so long, I hoped that he was safe. A year went by and there was still nothing heard from him, until my mum got a WhatsApp message from a random lady claiming to be pregnant. She said she was trying to locate her number from local neighbours and communities in Zambia till she got my mums number from a relative. She explained that she was carrying her son's child and that she was almost due to give birth. We couldn't believe it, even though we hadn't heard from Chimufa, we knew he was okay because he had found someone to be without there. The lady explained that their relationship ended before she knew she was pregnant and didn't know where he set off to. My mum was adamant on finding out if it was true… If it was really his child so we waited till the baby was born. It was really his child.

There were days when the silence was deafening. Not hearing from my brother tore me apart, the constant wonder of whether he was okay. But in the midst of that pain, there was a glimmer of hope - he had become a father. My heart was full knowing he had a child. Mum stepped up in the most incredible way. She got another day job to make sure the mother of the child lacked for nothing, sending money over to Zambia for essentials like food. She managed to secure a place for her to stay. It wasn't a palace, but it was enough for now. From nappies to baby clothes, Mum made sure the baby had what's needed.

Reaching out across borders was a different kind of challenge. Talking to the authorities felt like hitting a brick wall. They dangled information in front of us, expecting money in return. And if you didn't play their game, they shut you out. It's heart breaking to think some are so desperate that they'll exploit others' pain just to make a buck. But that's the world we live in. Some folks, struggling themselves, can be driven to make choices that hurt others.

Lost in Shadows, Reborn in Hope. Embracing a New Beginning.

It was a girl, she gave birth to my beautiful niece and named her 'Chimuka'. From that day I found purpose in life, a meaning to strive for greatness. A reason to keep living - to make Chimuka happy, loved, and safe. Every time I seen a photo of her, I smiled, she had big brown eyes, and a cute button nose.

I was motivated to build a life for myself, I used all my pain and strength into everything I pursued. I knew that one day I'd be successful, and I'd look after Chimuka, and I'd hope to find my brother Chimufa. I looked forward to finally being reunited with Benjamin, and that Mweeka would find the heart to reconnect with his little sister.

As I continued my journey as a young entrepreneur, the path was anything but smooth. It was rocky, very rocky. Just when I thought I had it all figured out, an unexpected twist loomed on the horizon...

END

This is a true story written by Donny Kkeiko, a triumphant entrepreneur, who penned this book to unveil the

challenges she encountered and her journey to triumph over them.

Stay tuned for the second Book.

Please consider sharing your thoughts by reviewing the book on platforms such as Amazon or Goodreads.

Printed in Great Britain
by Amazon